#MTPGA: 12 Things Christians Can Do Right Now

Dr. Mike Spaulding

Praise for #MTPGA: 12 Things Christians Can Do Right Now

"The Word of God well understood and religiously obeyed is the shortest route to spiritual perfection. Nothing less than a whole Bible can make a whole Christian."

—A. W. Tozer

In an age of information overload and the ability to conduct deep research into the Word of God with a push of a button, the modern Church is suffering from spiritual malnutrition. This spiritual phenomenon was not created by an absence of preaching. Rather, it has manifested in our generation through the preaching of another gospel and the pseudo-spiritual cotton candy of the Laodicean Church. In Dr. Michael Spaulding's new book, he releases a clarion call for those engaged in the holy task of ministering the Word to return to biblicity. For the Church to thrive in the days ahead, it must be continually fed with both the milk and meat of the Word. It is time for all of us to throw off our sugar addiction to the pablum of Babylon and make the preaching great again!

Dr. Michael K. Lake, author of *The Shinar Directive: Preparing the Way for the Son of Perdition*, and *The Sheeriyth Imperative: Empowering the Remnant to Overcome the Gates of Hell*.

America is in a Code Blue Moral and Spiritual Crisis. Christians and conservatives can point their fingers at the liberal left all they want. But ultimately, our crisis is a crisis of faith and obedience to God that only the Remnant Body of Christ can reverse. Pastor Mike Spaulding has provided not only an urgent call to action but, more importantly, a clear and concise template to make the pulpit great again! This book should be required reading for every pastor in America!

Gregg Jackson, national bestselling author of *40 Rules to Help Boys Become Men, 40 Things to Teach Your Children Before You Die*, & *Conservative Comebacks to Liberal Lies*

"My brother in Christ Dr. Mike Spaulding is quite simply a brilliant man and a man of God. He has a heart and vision to see significant changes happen in these last days within the modern church to help guide her out of the ditch and back onto the narrow path of holiness. He wants to see the church experience the presence of God speaking through his under shepherds from the pulpits, instead of hearing from those popular type motivational speakers disguised as pastors who today can give an entire sermon without even mentioning the Lord Jesus/Yeshua and the Holy Scriptures.

Caspar McCloud, Pastor of the Upper Room Fellowship, author of *Nothing is Impossible, What Was I Thinking*, and *Spiritual Encounter With the Shroud: Caspar McCloud Interviews with L.A. Marzulli*.

I was told recently that during the American War of Independence there was a Regiment that the British feared the most. They regularly made an appearance particularly on a Sunday and they were the preachers who preached from the bible who stood on the word of God to encourage the members of their congregations, in their fight against King George - no Taxation without representation.

The echoes of the past ring loudly in our ears on both sides of the pond, Brexit in the UK and the election of President Donald J Trump has revealed division within the Church. As my dear Brother in Christ Mike Spaulding, hastens to remind us that in Hebrews it talks about not moving on to solid food and still being on milk, milk signifying the fact that people wish to be entertained on a Sunday and not do real business with the living GOD.

It's not about making America or the UK great again it's about bringing people to salvation through repentance and forgiveness of sins not a side door of fuzzy-wuzzie feelings.

Dr. Mike Spaulding takes his best working boots and lends its full force to the back side of the Church of Laodicea and tells it to get its act together.

I'm **Mark Sutherland** Producer of *Between Lambs and Lions* https://www.youtube.com/watch?v=7hMQbvJP6HM and I fully endorse this message - Make American Pulpits Great Again and while you're at it the UK's too!

In *Make the Pulpit Great Again*, Dr. Mike Spaulding has addressed some of the gravest ills plaguing the American pulpit. Only through a policy of complacency and compromise adopted by the nation's pastors has the once-great United States ceded the moral high ground and set the standard for the rest of the world in pornography, addiction, perversion, and the murder of untold millions killed in state-sponsored, taxpayer-funded abortion mills. The words in Dr. Spaulding's book contain the secret to restoring this country to her former glory. For if we are ever to make America great again, we must first have a national call to repentance by our church leaders; we must make the pulpit great again.

Mark Goodwin Best Selling Author of *The Economic Collapse Chronicles, The Days of Noah, The Days of Elijah, Seven Cows Ugly and Gaunt,* and *Ava's Crucible.*

Pastor Mike Spaulding, my great friend and brother in Christ, has delivered a timely message for American Christians directly from the Word of God. In a time of undeniably great division and monumental historical significance, when so many can without much effort identify dozens of major problems that our society faces, we find ourselves long on complaints but short on solutions. Pastor Mike pulls no punches in his matter of fact analysis and encourages believers of all stations to press in to God, to stand up, and to be counted for the glory of the name of Jesus.

My prayer is that this would serve as a signpost to believers and unbelievers alike, pointing them back to the one true God and to the path of life that He desires us to walk in this generation. May God speak to you, strengthen you, and give you the faith to grow in Christ and attain spiritual maturity through these pages and the scriptures they draw upon!

Steven Menking, Host and Senior Editor, *On the Objective*

DEDICATION

This book is dedicated to the love of my life, the bride of my youth, the hallelujah choir of the sound booth, my wife Kathy. Words fall short of describing all you mean to me. May God continue to richly bless you in all you set your hands and mind to do in His service.

Mike Spaulding

TABLE OF CONTENTS

Foreword

"Where do I go?"

I have heard this question, and its variants, more times than I can mention; where do I find a church that teaches God's Word? Can you point me to a church I can trust? Do you know a church that is theologically sound?

When this primary question is normalized, and increasingly it is becoming so, then a certain outcome or effect is anticipated. It can be found in the following statement: "I'm a Christian, but I don't go anywhere, anymore." Sadly, this is a sentence I hear all too often. It is one that my friend, Pastor Mike Spaulding, hears as well.

There are reasons why this shift is happening, internal causes within the Christian world – often well intended – that have, nevertheless, eroded the purpose of the pulpit. In turn, those in the pews have found themselves drifting out of churches. Or, as is often the case, staying and being fed on milk and not meat. Mike explores those issues, important in giving us context.

However, if you think this book is about placing blame on one group over another, pastors versus laymen, you're sorely mistaken. Mike makes it very clear that cults of personality are a "blight upon the Church not a cause of celebration." This is not about making "pastors great again." And those in the pews? A necessary challenge is put forth to move past spiritual infancy, to quit focusing on the personal "I" and selfist "Me" – What can *I* get out of this? How is this relevant to *me*?

Could it be that we are following models given by the world? The question is rhetorical. A Christian re-focus is thus necessary, from the podium to the Sunday School classroom to the sanctuary. But the re-focus needs to go deeper still, from the church to the home to the heart.

And the time isn't too soon. As Mike reminds us in chapter 4, "The time in which we live today is the absolute worst time for Christians to be sleep walking through life." He rightly raises the question: "How do Christians expect to navigate through life without a sure foundation of the Word?"

Unpacking twelve key action points, from putting on God's armor – emphasizing that it is *God's armor*, His protection afforded to His children – to prayer and fasting, understanding the times, studying the Word, strengthening the family, and more, this book offers insights into what you can do *right now*.

But hold on: This is not so much a *to do list* as a *to change list*. More programs and more business isn't the answer. What Mike is ultimately pointing to, is a change of heart and soul and mind, with actions reflecting that change, building on it, and then pouring God's love and truth back into the Church and beyond. Pulpits will be great again when we recognize the greatness of God, and take our responsibilities as Ambassadors for Jesus Christ seriously. Each of us are to be God's *truth tellers*, proclaiming His truth in word and deed, and *living* His truth in our daily walk.

That Pastor Spaulding wrote this book isn't surprising. For those like myself, who have spent time with Mike in conversation, his heart for the Church is well known. Long before his fingers ever hit the keyboard, Mike has had a God-given desire to see the pulpit made great again – not for the aggrandizement of pastors, and not for the personal happiness of the congregants.

The pulpit must be made great again, for and to, the *glory of God*.

Carl Teichrib

-

ACKNOWLEDGMENTS

I am grateful for the many brothers and sisters of the faith who have come into my life over the last thirty-five years. But I especially want to thank Pastor Wes Kunztman, my first pastor, who gently nurtured me as a new believer, Pastor Tom Brodbeck, who took a young man full of fire and passion and taught him to be a servant, and Pastor Gene McBride, who taught me much about what it means to be a man of God. I think of all of you often and thank God for the roles you played in my formative years.

INTRODUCTION

This book is in my view long overdue. It is overdue for two reasons. First, is that I have thought for many years that a book addressing the subject of the Church generally and pastors specifically is needed. However, it was only recently however, that the idea for "#MTPGA: 12 Things Christians Can Do Right Now," came to me. As a pastor I am interested in the body of Christ and those things that affect it. Second, the people of the remnant body of Christ need to know that they are not alone. Indeed the remnant body of Christ is the real Church, and the real Church is needed today like never before.

I have become increasingly alarmed by the decadence that is seeping into every aspect of American life and consequently the Church. I have often wondered out loud, where is the Church? More specifically, where are the pastors, the ministry leaders, and the individual Christians? Why is there no outcry over the many evils that have invaded America?

I was reminded that there are a handful of faithful pastors and ministry leaders who continue to serve God faithfully by decrying the many evils that have come upon us. On the other hand, I also realized that except for a very small remnant, these faithful servants of God are ignored by the majority of professing believers.

The book of Jeremiah clearly explains the predicament we face today clearly. Hear the words of God pronouncing judgment upon His people Israel in 6:16-20:

Thus says the LORD,
"Stand by the ways and see and ask for the ancient paths,
Where the good way is, and walk in it;
and you will find rest for your souls.
But they said, 'We will not walk *in it.*'
"And I set watchmen over you, *saying,*
'Listen to the sound of the trumpet!'
But they said, 'We will not listen.'
"Therefore hear, O nations,
And know, O congregation, what is among them.
"Hear, O earth: behold, I am bringing disaster on this people,
The fruit of their plans,
Because they have not listened to My words,
And as for My law, they have rejected it also.
"For what purpose does frankincense come to Me from Sheba
And the sweet cane from a distant land?
Your burnt offerings are not acceptable
and your sacrifices are not pleasing to Me."[1]

In the book of Jeremiah God called His people to return to Him in true worship, obedience, and service. By their actions they told Him they would not do those things. This is one of many reasons that God called Israel an obstinate and stiff-necked people. Sadly, Christians are doing the same thing today. Too many individuals that call themselves Christians are such in name only. The reality is that many people who claim to be believers are really little more than practical atheists. Their lifestyles deny God His rightful place in their lives every day.

The problem for the Israelites was that they heeded the wrong voices. The priests charged with spiritual oversight were not speaking God's truth.

Those Israelites who were faithful to speak God's truth such as Jeremiah were ignored, threatened, and worse. The same thing is being repeated today in the Church. Many pastors who speak the truth today find

---

[1] Unless otherwise stated all Scripture references are from The New American Standard Bible Expanded Edition, 1995 Update (La Habra, CA: Lockman Foundation).

themselves without a job quickly. Others are simply ignored and marginalized because of their perceived "radical attitude." Fact is Christians will not tolerate being made to feel "uncomfortable" by the truths of the Bible and certainly not by the accompanying conviction and direction of the Holy Spirit.

Notice that in the Jeremiah passage cited above God sets His watchmen in place to warn the people of their spiritual condition (Jeremiah 6:17) and to lead them on the "ancient paths" and the "good way" (Jeremiah 6:16). Disastrously, the people respond "we will not walk in it." What are the ancient paths and the good way? The Bible is God's revelation to us and is the path we should always follow. The Bible is a light for our path.[2] It is in the Bible that we are commanded to love Jesus by obeying Him. It is the Scripture that teaches us to pick up our cross and follow Jesus.

Today we have denominations discarding the Bible entirely, changing their doctrines and their teaching to reflect their capitulation to cultural forces, and in the process creating carnal, fleshly, man-pleasing doctrines (Matthew 15:9) that are nothing more than doctrines of demons (1 Timothy 4:1). God's people are being deliberately led astray.

God condemned this same behavior in the Old Testament. There are dozens of instances of God's condemnation of shepherds that led His people astray. Consider these examples just from the book of Jeremiah:

- For the shepherds have become stupid and have not sought the Lord; Therefore they have not prospered, and all their flock is scattered (Jeremiah 10:21).

- Many shepherds have ruined my vineyard, they have trampled down My field; they have made My pleasant field A desolate wilderness (Jeremiah 12:10).

- Woe to the shepherds who are destroying and scattering the sheep of My pasture! declares the Lord. Therefore thus says the Lord God of Israel concerning the shepherds who are tending My people: "You have scattered My flock and driven them away, and

---

[2] Psalm 119:105

have not attended to them; behold, I am about to attend to you for the evil of your deeds," declares the Lord (Jeremiah 23:1-2).

- My people have become lost sheep; Their shepherds have led them astray. They have made them turn aside *on* the mountains; They have gone along from mountain to hill and have forgotten their resting place (Jeremiah 50:6).

American Christians are suffering because of the unfaithful shepherds in our midst. The Church's mission has become a putrid mix of social, cultural, and politically correct vomit because of these false shepherds. It is time that faithful pastors, ministry leaders, and individual Christians unite to become a force for God in these perilous days. The fields are white for harvest but the laborers are few.

It is time for Christians to "Make The Pulpit Great Again" (#MTPGA). Do not mishear me friends, I am not suggesting that we make pastors great. The cult of personality that exists today related to "rock star" pastors is a blight upon the Church not a cause of celebration. What I am suggesting is that we make the role of shepherd great again. God still calls people to be His undershepherds, to teach His people His Word, and to educate as well as train them for the work of ministry (Ephesians 4:11-12).

What will that take? It will take the remnant body of Christ pulling in the same direction. It will take the remnant body of Christ holding pastors and one another accountable for faithfulness to the task of feeding sheep. I am stating plainly that until or unless Christians realize that they must hold up the banner of truth and righteousness as a clear rallying point, the Church will remain ineffective.

We must also come to terms with our own complacency and complicity. We must get on our faces before God and repent of our callousness and apathy. Christianity in America in many instances is a bloated, malnourished, spiritually starving entity that has been lulled to sleep by materialism, false assurances of God's protection against the horrors visited upon our brothers and sisters in other nations every day, and the wide spread belief that the government of the United States is a friend of the

Church. I earnestly pray that the Church wakes up to the reality of the certain calamity that awaits it if it does not repent and seek God once again.

Some may say but Pastor Mike, the Church cannot be overcome. Ultimately that is correct. God's plans will not be thwarted but you will not find God using people who refuse to answer the call to engage the culture, to stand firm against the onslaught of evil, and to speak righteously to an unrighteous generation. God will simply set those people aside and they will live feeble, unfulfilled, and unrewarding lives that do not honor their King.

I believe there is strength in numbers and so we must assemble together like-minded believers who will cast off the cultural allures to focus on the work of God in our time. What might that work be? Our great work includes as a first priority taking care of our families that constitute the body of Christ. We must start where our own Jerusalem is and only when our local body is whole and healthy should we look for a Samaria. Certainly it includes - and I would argue starts with - stopping the satanic slaughter of our unborn children. Abortion is a blood offering to Satan. Stop allowing Christians to refer to it as a choice as if they were picking something off a menu for lunch.

Won't you join me in this great effort? Let's Make The Pulpit Great Again so we will be found standing with the shepherds that are honoring God and proclaiming Him to be the only answer to the death spiral that the world is in. Let's Make The Pulpit Great Again as we refuse to accept lame, cotton candy sermonettes designed to distract the sheep from the severity of the issues we face. Let's Make The Pulpit Great Again so that God's people, the body of Christ, can become a ferocious warrior that unflinchingly engages the enemy in every venue he is found. Let's demand that the whole counsel of God ring out from our pulpits and our churches such that Christians are set afire once again with the passion for lost souls that sent men and women throughout the world in generations past to proclaim that only Jesus saves!

But salvation from the penalty of sin is only the beginning. Let's Make The Pulpit Great Again so that Christians are moved beyond virtual morality into actual life-saving missions to abortion clinics, to prisons, jails, half-way houses, and drug infested neighborhoods. Let's go to the least among us and by the authority and power in the name of Jesus declare that the captives are freed! America will never be great unless the Church discovers anew the power of Jesus Christ to heal the sick and cast out the demonic hordes that have taken up residence in myriads across this nation. The Church will not be great until it focuses on God alone as the reason for its existence and the content of its message. This campaign starts in the pulpits of America!

Pastor Mike
#MTPGA
February 22, 2018

Chapter 1 – Realize Who You Are: Why Are We Suffering From An Identity Crisis?

But you are a Chosen Race, a Royal Priesthood, a Holy Nation, a people for God's own possession, so that you may proclaim the excellencies of Him who has called you out of darkness into His marvelous light. 1 Peter 2:9

When reality smacks up against perception it can be a sobering experience. Statistics from the Barna Group indicate that professing Christians hold to the same views as their unsaved friends and neighbors in the categories of viewing pornography, maintaining legalized abortion, and in supporting same-sex unions.[3]

Pornography is a plague upon every person it entraps, disrupting the natural affections and distorting the expectations people place upon their spouse's. Pornographic images burn themselves into the memory banks of the mind

---

[3] For stats on pornography among professing believers go here - https://www.cnsnews.com/news/article/penny-starr/pornography-use-among-self-identified-christians-largely-mirrors-national Accessed March 8, 2018. For stats on abortion go here - https://www.christianpost.com/news/70-of-women-who-get-abortions-identify-as-christians-survey-finds-150937/ Accessed March 8, 2018. For stats on same-sex unions go here - https://www.reuters.com/article/us-usa-lgbt-marriage/evangelical-christians-becoming-less-opposed-to-gay-marriage-poll-finds-idUSKBN19I2MU Accessed March 8, 2018.

and the enemy of God's people throws them up on the big screen every opportunity he has. Social scientists and law enforcement professionals agree that many crimes are directly linked to the perpetrator's consumption of pornographic material.[4]

Abortion, for all the euphemisms people use to blunt the truth of what it is, is still the murder of unborn human beings. The barbaric practice of abortion - regardless of the type, scope, or process - is still a modern day blood offering to Satan.

Same-sex marriage is an oxymoron. Marriage has been ordained by God since Genesis as a union between a man and a woman. Adultery is not "having a fling" or an "affair." It is a violation of the covenant a man and woman swear to uphold before God as their witness.

Since all of this is true and attested to by the inerrant Word of God, why do so many professing believers struggle to overcome these spiritual, physical, and emotional traps? When the data is available for everyone to see, when wrecked lives, utterly devastated marriages, and children in crisis are evidence of the dangers of the actions captured statistically above, why do Christians of all people continue to believe they won't be touched by their participation in them?

How is it possible that people who have the Holy Spirit of God living in them can engage in such behavior on a routine basis? How is it possible that people who profess to follow Jesus Christ practice at nearly the same percentages as their unbelieving family, friends, and co-workers the things listed above? These statistics alert us to the fact that the holiness and righteousness Christians are empowered to exhibit is not accomplished by many thousands who profess faith in Christ. Worse still, apparently many are perfectly fine with that.

Friends, something is terribly wrong with the type of Christianity being manifested by a large segment of professing believers today. How has the

---

[4] Statistics available at https://fightthenewdrug.org/the-disturbing-link-between-porn-and-sex-crimes/ Accessed February 25, 2018.

message of the Bible become so convoluted as to give cover for these egregious behaviors and manifold others?

I believe that one of many reasons professing Christians engage in ungodly and sinful behavior is that they have become convinced that God loves them no matter what and that His primary concern for them is their happiness. Thus, if God wants what makes us happy, then an unexpected pregnancy can be terminated. After all, God knows we are not ready to be a parent and it would be a shame to try to raise a child when the timing isn't right.

Now, readers should be asking themselves at this point, where does anyone who reads the Bible come up with the idea that God's primary concern is for people's happiness? You are correct to ask that question, and I believe you already know the answer. It's not found in the Bible but it is taught by many pastors as their stock and trade. Appealing to people emotionally is big business in the Church today. Encouraging people to chase things natural to the flesh while cloaking it in quasi-biblical garb, only feeds the beast of unencumbered ego, unfettered desire, and unfulfilled expectation.

Overcoming sinful behavior is not accomplished by incessantly repeating to people that God loves them so much and will continue to love them through their sinful behavior. While God does indeed love, God forbid we wield that card as a license to sin. Let's apply practically this posture of absolute hypergrace and the justification of sin to drug addiction. How are we helping people by telling them as they are shooting a deadly poison into their veins even up to overdose and death that God loves them? Stop that! You and I both know that instead we must intervene and do whatever it takes to assist someone in stopping any such destructive behavior, even by employing what is commonly called tough love.

The truth is that pastors are creating train wrecks in believer's lives through the things they teach week by week. Calling people to holy and righteous living is so 1950's in the minds of many today. Simply teaching the Bible is now viewed as backward and out of step with modern society. Nonetheless, here is a truth we must accept and press, abandoning straightforward Bible teaching has opened a Pandora's Box that we cannot shut. I believe this is why so many Christians engage in the ungodly behaviors listed above. They are not hearing the Bible taught as the power of God unto salvation and godly living. It is instead seen as a collection of good moral guidelines that might happen to be reasonable recommendations if they are ever needed.

Adding to this clear dilemma is the fact that discipleship and church discipline are also disregarded. If we are taking seriously the Scriptural command to make disciples of every nation, by teaching them the words of Jesus – while being lovingly confrontational as part of our corporate life together - then these snares of the enemy would not be so successful.

What Christians need today are pastors who will say "the deeds of the flesh are…" and who will back this up with action. Christians are as the Apostle Peter reminds us, ". . . a Chosen Race, a Royal Priesthood, a Holy Nation, a people for God's own possession, so that you may proclaim the excellencies of Him who has called you out of darkness into His marvelous light." Because Christians, those who have trusted in Christ's atoning work on Calvary's cross for the forgiveness of their sins, have been called out of the darkness to walk in the light that is Jesus Christ, we must deny darkness any and every opportunity to manifest in us or in those we love.

Only when we are walking in the light of Jesus Christ can we proclaim His excellencies. Our testimony to what God has done in our lives is a very important aspect of remembering who we are. God says many things about His sons and daughters in the Bible. We can encourage one another with those things.

Are we suffering from an identity crisis as believers today? Indeed we are.

Too many Christians do not understand who they truly are in Christ because they've never been taught. They are dragon slayers. Christians are meant to be people of renown or at least a peculiar people when contrasted with the culture at large.[5] Wisdom and courage are to be our constant companions. An unflinching devotion to Christ is of primary importance in our lives. Christ said that our love for Him would be demonstrated by our

---

[5] 1 Peter 2:9 in the KJV.

obedience to what He commands. Obedience to Christ leads to blessings from Him, assurance of who He is and a constant experience of His power working in us and through us.

We cannot occupy until Christ comes again if we do not even know that we are even in His Army. How do we start to regain what has been lost to the deceptive teaching of hirelings and modern day motivational speakers masquerading as pastors? We start right here and now by reclaiming our spiritual God-given heritage.

First, we must throw off the effeminate pseudo-identity that culture has foisted upon us. Why do we allow pagans, heretics, and the unsaved masses in the media, government indoctrination centers (public schools), and social media behemoths to dictate to us who we are in Christ? Men, it is time to be real men. Lead your families with godly vision and holy fire. Love your wife and give her your best, not the crumbs left over after doing everything else that needs done in your day. Protect your children from the ravenous wolves of secularism, the anointed high priests of our government education propaganda system and from the evil of media in all its ubiquitous forms. These are slithering serpents that brainwash people until they become mindless zombies repeating the ungodly drivel of progressivism which is only progressive in its march away from God.

Second, we must become better at listening carefully to the Holy Spirit. He will lead us day by day if we will take the time to listen. How important is this? Consider just a few of the things the Bible tells us about living by the power of and under the anointing of the Holy Spirit.

> Peter *said* to them, "Repent, and each of you be baptized in the name of Jesus Christ for the forgiveness of your sins; and you will receive the gift of the Holy Spirit. (Acts 2:38)

> Jesus answered, "Truly, truly, I say to you, unless one is born of water and the Spirit he cannot enter into the kingdom of God. (John 3:5)

> It is the Spirit who gives life; the flesh profits nothing; the words

that I have spoken to you are spirit and are life. (John 6:63)

If we live by the Spirit, let us also walk by the Spirit. (Galatians 5:25)

for we are the *true* circumcision, who worship in the Spirit of God and glory in Christ Jesus and put no confidence in the flesh, (Philippians 3:3)

God is spirit, and those who worship Him must worship in spirit and truth. (John 4:24)

The reality of our new life in Christ is that we are provided with all that we need day by day to live obediently to the Father by the Holy Spirit in us. The Holy Spirit will always lead us into righteousness and will never lead us into error. The Holy Spirit will always lead us toward the fight and never into cowardice.

Third, we must become people of prayer. Husbands pray for your wives.[6] Wives love your husbands, support and respect them. I encourage wives to pray[7] Proverbs 4:20-27 over your husbands daily. It states clearly the importance of listening to the Word of God and allowing it to govern the mind, soul, and heart.

> My son, give attention to my words;
> Incline your ear to my sayings.
> Do not let them depart from your sight;
> Keep them in the midst of your heart.
> For they are life to those who find them
> and health to all their body.
> Watch over your heart with all diligence,
> for from it *flow* the springs of life.
> Put away from you a deceitful mouth
> and put devious speech far from you.

---

[6] See Chapter 9 for specific reasons why men must pray for their wives.
[7] *Covering Your Husband in Prayer 31 Days* available here - http://intothekingsgarden.blogspot.com/2013/05/wives-pray-for-your-husband.html Accessed February 26, 2018.

Let your eyes look directly ahead
and let your gaze be fixed straight in front of you.
Watch the path of your feet
and all your ways will be established.
Do not turn to the right nor to the left;
Turn your foot from evil.

Finally, plumb the depths of the Bible together as men, women, and children. Stop the misinformed segregation of our young people into their "teen" or "youth" groups and learn the wonder of our great God together. Make sure you are teaching your children the Bible and not a publisher's watered down version of Bible stories.

Demand and only support shepherds who are faithful to proclaim the whole truth of the Bible. Friends, it is in the pages of the Bible that we must learn who God is and what He says about us. Our identity is found in God's Word, in His heart for us, and in the myriad pictures of His love for us. Remember and cherish this.

A word of caution here – this is not a call to a "witch hunt" or the creation of a new cadre of Pharisees who sit in judgment of the shepherds God has called. It is a call to support and encourage faithful men who teach and preach and give of themselves for the benefit of God's people. You should know the difference between men who need to be dismissed because they are not called of God and men who need to be supported. We are called to treat one another with love and respect.[8]

When we understand who we are in Christ, the resources that are ours by spiritual birthright, and the power that living a life of obedience yields to our earthly benefit, we will regain our true identity and rise up in unison to advance the Light that is Jesus Christ.

---

[8] Mark 12:29-31; John 13:34-35; Romans 13:8; Galatians 5:13; Ephesians 4:2; 1 Thessalonians 3:12; for example.

Chapter 2 – Be Wise and Blameless: But Grow Up

Behold, I send you out as sheep in the midst of wolves; so be shrewd as serpents and innocent as doves. Jesus Christ as recorded in Matthew 10:16

One of the major themes of the Apostle Paul's letters is the need for believers to grow up. Paul was not suggesting that Christians were childish but rather that they were like children when it came to their professed faith. He was saying that many believers had not grown spiritually, even though much time had passed since their profession of faith. There was no evidence of growth in knowledge, in understanding the implications of living for Christ, or in manifestation of the fruits of repentance, and Paul stated matter-of-factly that there was no excuse for their lack of spiritual growth.

The apostle wrote to the Corinthians:

> I gave you milk to drink, not solid food; for you were not yet able *to receive it*. Indeed, even now you are not yet able. (1 Corinthians 3:7)

The writer to the Hebrews likewise encouraged his readers to grow in their faith:

> For though by this time you ought to be teachers, you have need again for someone to teach you the elementary principles of the oracles of God, and you have come to need milk and not solid food. (Hebrews 5:12)

With few exceptions the same climate of spiritual infancy is visible in the modern American Church. We see many churches full of happy congregants willing to spend a couple of hours fellowshipping, listening to the latest contemporary music performed on stage, and even receiving a 20-30 minute "talk" by a very articulate speaker. Yes I know, I just described the stereotypical Saturday or Sunday church service for a large segment of Christendom.

You might be asking yourself what exactly is wrong about the procedure I just described. What more should we expect? Actually we should expect much more than what is common fare today in much of the Church.

First, my expectation is that when the body of Christ meets it does so with an expectation of hearing the Bible taught clearly and passionately. The pastor should teach from the Bible and makes his points the passage under consideration directly presents. Trying to focus on application and relevancy to the exclusion of the themes presented is a sure recipe for missing the point. What is the true purpose here? We must allow the Holy Spirit to do the work that He does. Bible teachers should teach and permit the Holy Spirit to make the appropriate application of the text to each listener's heart. I can't number the times that after a sermon several people will tell me that they heard this or that and someone else will say they heard so and so. Everyone had heard the same sermon, the exact same words, but the Holy Spirit had quickened different portions and spoke uniquely to each believer's heart. Don't miss this: we should not lose sleep over trying to force a point from a particular passage in order to make it relevant. Trying to be relevant in my view makes you irrelevant because you are attempting to do the work of the Holy Spirit.[9] A healthy body of believers feasts regularly on solid Bible teaching.

Second, I expect that when the body of Christ meets together we actually focus on God the Father, God the Son, and God the Holy Spirit when we sing songs that we call worship. I believe our music should reflect a reverence for God, a thankful heart attitude for the salvation we have received from Him.[10] Jesus condemned ritual and rote behavior that passed as worship in His day.[11]

I know in today's church climate speaking up about the music selection puts one on thin ice with many. Let me say that I'm not adverse to most contemporary musical expressions as long as they focus on God. Why this qualification? It is needed because many songs being sung today in church worship services are nothing more than therapeutic ballads to self. Your first clue that music that should facilitate the worship of God is nothing more than another song is the focus on "I" in the lyrics and a near total absence of mentioning the Lord. You are not worshipping God by focusing on self. Singing songs about everything we are pledging to do is not worship of the Father.

Third, I expect that when the body of Christ meets there will be a good portion of time spent praying corporately for the needs of that local body, their families, and the people in their spheres – be they friends, neighbors, or co-workers. I expect that prayer time should also be focused on others. Praying for our cities, America, and for our persecuted brethren elsewhere is something that the body should be doing consistently and fervently. Newsflash folks – your time is God's time when you meet together. Remember that you are there for Him. Therefore, if that means He decides to highjack the carefully planned schedule and keep you in a spirit of prayer, intercession, supplication, and thanksgiving for the entire morning then glory to God! For He is among His people!

---

[9] See Chapter 4 for some of the many works the Holy Spirit does for, in, and through the believer.

[10] Psalm 103 is an example of what it means to worship God – with heart, soul, mind, and strength.

[11] See Mark 7:6-8 where Jesus tells the religious leaders that they "honor Me with their lips, but their hearts are far from Me. But in vain do they worship Me, teaching as doctrines the precepts of men."

Grow Christian Grow!

As I mentioned earlier the writer to the Hebrews makes no secret of the fact that Christians must take action in order to grow in spiritual maturity.

> Therefore leaving the elementary teaching about the Christ, let us press on to maturity, not laying again a foundation of repentance from dead works and of faith toward God. (Hebrews 6:1)

Notice that the writer tells us that we are to "press on." This means we are to be actively involved in our maturation process. It is sad to see Christians who believe that spiritual maturity is merely a process of osmosis. Those individuals believe that if they are faithful in their church attendance, read a chapter a day in their Bibles, and pray before they go to sleep at night, then they will automatically grow into a mature Christian.

Here's some bad news for those people: you don't grow without being an active participant in what God describes as the process for growth. In the passage above the writer to the Hebrews says we are to leave the elementary things behind and highlights the need to progress beyond the elementary teaching about the Christ. In other words, there is much more to learn about Jesus and to live for Jesus than that He died on Calvary's cross as transcendentally magnificent as that truth might be. He also rose from the dead, appeared to hundreds, ascended to heaven, sent the Comforter, and calls people into a faith relationship with Him even today.

It may be in vogue today to forsake theology in favor of lukewarm pep talks and the warm-fuzzies. But imprecise thinking will not draw you closer to Christ nor provide the impetus for spiritual growth of the kind the Bible describes. The "meatier" issues of the faith are not apprehended by lazy Christians.

Why must we do all of this? I call your attention to this chapter's Scripture, Matthew 10:16. What is the context of Jesus' words? Spiritual warfare is clearly in view. He says definitively that He sends out His people to the wolves of this world. This eternal truth applies to us today even as it applied to the disciples His words dispatched as they were first uttered.

You might be thinking that Jesus hasn't sent you out to fight the wolves because you're just a Sunday school teacher or a Christian without structured ministry inside an institutional church. Let me remind you of a couple of things. We are all called to the battle in some form or another – and often in several forms simultaneously. The Ephesian Christians were informed that they were Christ's workmanship. He created them to do good works prepared beforehand for them to engage in.[12]

What was Jesus' expectation of the twelve when He sent them out as recorded in Matthew 10? Turn in your Bible's to Matthew 10:1 and read the good works Jesus has prepared you to engage in. I can almost hear the protestations now. But Mike, you can't possibly be serious! That was for a specific assignment in a specific time as a means to authenticate the ministry of Jesus and His disciples. Jesus really doesn't expect us to do that today. I've heard that objection many times before.

Contrast what Jesus trained the disciples to do with what transpires in a good many churches across America today. Many shepherds have become content to teach you the rudimentary truths of the Gospel and most believers have accepted those truths as all there is to being a Christian. Some shepherds try to lull their flocks into a sense of adventure without leaving the sanctuary by teaching series on edgy subjects like "having your best sex now," or "how to have a marriage all your friends will envy," or some other type of superfluous nonsense. That is not to say that the Word of God doesn't have important wisdom about intimacy and relationship. Simply put, Bible teaching must be line upon line and precept upon precept instead of something proffered to catch the eye. The holiness and power of God's presence is the best way to get someone's attention and focus it where the attention is most worthily placed.

Let me be bold with you here. If you are in a "church" that uses props, lighting, visually stimulating special effects and rock star quality bands to entertain then you are likely growing in the wrong direction. And if you are growing in the wrong direction then you are growing in ways that are detrimental to your spiritual health and eventually to your earthly well-

---

[12] Ephesians 2:10

being. Growing thorns and thistles in your life will eventually lead to a scorched field.[13]

Here is my point – there is so much more victory available to Christians in this life than most imagine. There is so much more power available to us as blood-bought, redeemed, born-again, spirit-filled believers than many comprehend. Most Christians today have settled for Christianity-lite. It's less filling, affords lots of leisure time, and can be managed quite easily.

The world under the influence of our mortal enemy will not break a sweat in destroying any believer who has not grown up into a mature man or woman. The Bible describes our adversary as a roaring lion for a reason.[14] Therefore we must be constantly on alert and able to stand firm through our understanding the power of the Holy Spirit in us.

May we press on to break through the elementary teachings of the Scriptures to attain the status of workmen who are not ashamed!

---

[13] Hebrews 6:8
[14] 1 Peter 5:8-9

Chapter 3 – Be Bold and Courageous: Fearlessness

"Have I not commanded you? Be strong and courageous! Do not tremble or be dismayed, for the LORD your God is with you wherever you go." Joshua 1:9

What do Cleveland Brown's running back Leroy Kelly, New York Yankee's first baseman Babe Dahlgren, and Los Angeles Lakers center Vlade Divac have in common? If you guessed that each followed a legend in their particular sport you are correct. Kelly took Jim Brown's spot in the Browns backfield, Dahlgren took over for Lou Gehrig, and Divac replaced the retired Kareem Abdul Jabbar.

So what? Who cares about sports figures, particularly relatively obscure ones? I think Joshua had an even greater assignment when he assumed the unenviable position of following Moses in leading the Israelites. I can't even begin to imagine what that would be like. However, there was one thing that Joshua possessed that none of the people listed above possessed. That one thing was God's leading and direction to be strong and courageous, for He was with him wherever he went. Talk about lifting your confidence!

One of the many things that churches and church leadership lack today is an appreciation for the promises of God. Consider just these few:

James 4:7 - Submit therefore to God. Resist the devil and he will flee from you.

1 John 1:9 - If we confess our sins, He is faithful and righteous to forgive us our sins and to cleanse us from all unrighteousness.

Deuteronomy 31:8 - The LORD is the one who goes ahead of you; He will be with you. He will not fail you or forsake you. Do not fear or be dismayed.

Isaiah 54:17 - No weapon that is formed against you will prosper; and every tongue that accuses you in judgment you will condemn. This is the heritage of the servants of the LORD, and their vindication is from Me, declares the LORD.

I could fill up many more pages with verses telling us clearly that God is with us to strengthen us for the difficulties we face in fulfilling the assignments He gives us. That being the case, why are so many individual Christians and so many churches weak and afraid when it comes to putting their faith to action? Could it be that they've never been taught the Word of God or heard their pastor encourage them to trust God for the provision of everything they need to be obedient to His calling upon their life?

I remember reading a book over 25 years ago that made what I considered after reflection a truly profound statement that resonates even more today. The author said that God is always working to accomplish His plans and that He is always working all around you. Therefore it is incumbent upon every believer to pray and ask God to show you where He is working and to seek to join Him in that work.

Friend, now consider this carefully: If God is always working around you and He reveals where He is working to you, then isn't that an invitation to join Him? Moreover, if God invites you to join Him then won't He provide everything you need to fulfill that assignment? Pastor Chuck Smith was fond of saying that where God guides God provides and it is just as true today as it was for Moses and Joshua.

Since God is omnipotent and willing to support His people in the work of His kingdom, why are there still so few laborers in the fields? If God reveals His work, calls Christians to the work, provides them with the necessary resources, and gives them strength as well as courage, then why are the laborers so few? Sheep will follow their shepherd. It is a law of nature. Is it possible that faith among Christians today is lacking because the shepherds of America are more concerned with being liked and well thought of in their communities than they are concerned about being faithful to God's call to be strong, courageous, and an effective conqueror of the darkness in the power and authority of Jesus name?

Since God issues His call to us, provides the necessary capacities for us to accomplish what He desires, and goes with us as we move forward into every new land, why is there such widespread apathy and outright refusal to go?

A.W. Tozer was a man for the ages. He was a pastor and prolific author who gave his thoughts on the church and Christianity without apology. Although he went to his glory in the early 1960's his words are just as timely today as they were then.

In a compilation of Tozer's writings, we find this evocative passage:

> If Christianity is to receive a rejuvenation, it must be by other means than any now being used. If the Church in the second half of this century is to recover from the injuries she suffered in the first half, there must appear a new type of preacher.

> Another kind of religious leader must arise among us. He must be of the old prophet type, a man who has seen visions of God and has heard a voice from the Throne. When he comes (and I pray God there will be not one but many), he will stand in flat contradiction to everything our smirking, smooth civilization holds dear.

> He will contradict, denounce and protest in the name of God and will earn the hatred and opposition of a large segment of Christendom. Such a man is likely to be lean, rugged, blunt-spoken and a little bit angry with the world.

> He will love Christ and the souls of men to the point of willingness
> to die for the glory of the One and the salvation of the other. But
> he will fear nothing that breathes with mortal breath.[15]

This captures the heart of the issue friends. There is a sore lack of
fearlessness within the body of Christ today, most glaringly and tragically in
the Christian pulpits of America. Oh but Mike, don't you know the day of
the fire-breathing preacher has passed like the dinosaur before it? Then I
say it is time to revive the fire-breathing shepherd again! But Mike, this kind
of pastor will not be liked by his peers and most Christians won't care for
someone like that!

What does the Apostle Paul think of those objections?

> As we have said before, so I say again now, if any man is preaching
> to you a gospel contrary to what you received, he is to be accursed!
> For am I now seeking the favor of men, or of God? Or am I
> striving to please men? If I were still trying to please men, I would
> not be a bond-servant of Christ. (Galatians 1:9-10)

Listen to me pastor, elder, deacon, or ministry leader. If your primary
concern is to please your congregants, your friends, your neighbors, or
anyone else other than God alone you are in rebellion to the One who
called you into the Gospel ministry. If you are thinking, "I don't preach, I
only lead a Bible study, so I'm not any of those things," so this standard
does not apply to me," then let me remind you of this:

> Therefore if anyone is in Christ, *he is* a new creature; the old things
> passed away; behold, new things have come. Now all *these* things
> are from God, who reconciled us to Himself through Christ and
> gave us the ministry of reconciliation, namely, that God was in
> Christ reconciling the world to Himself, not counting their
> trespasses against them, and He has committed to us the word of
> reconciliation. Therefore, we are ambassadors for Christ, as though

---

[15] This quote appears in *Tozer on Christian Leadership,* compiled by Ron Eggert (Camp Hill,
PA: Christian Publications, Inc), 2001, on the March 21 page. It originally was part of
Tozer's book, *The Size of the Soul: Principles OF Revival and Spiritual Growth,* compiled by Harry
Verploegh (Camp Hill, PA: Christian Publications Inc), 1992.

God were making an appeal through us; we beg you on behalf of Christ, be reconciled to God. He made Him who knew no sin *to be* sin on our behalf, so that we might become the righteousness of God in Him. (2 Corinthians 5:17-21)

Here is Tozer again:

> A prophet is one who knows his times and what God is trying to say to the people of his times.
>
> Today we need prophetic preachers – not preachers of prophecy merely, but preachers with a gift of prophecy. The word of wisdom is missing. We need the gift of discernment again in our pulpits. It is not ability to predict that we need, but the anointed eye, the power of spiritual penetration and interpretation, the ability to appraise the religious scene as viewed from God's position, and to tell us what is actually going on.
>
> What is needed desperately today is prophetic insight. Scholars can interpret the past; it takes prophets to interpret the present. Learning will enable a man to pass judgment on our yesterdays, but it requires a gift of clear seeing to pass sentence on our own day.[16]

My point here is that serving God, which all Christians are commanded to do, means that you will be like a fish out of water. You will stick out like a sore thumb. You will march to a different drummer. But enough of the clichés – you will look, act, and speak differently than the culture at large. You will be a man or woman alive with a passion to speak to people about the grand delusion that has enveloped much of the Church and consequently much of what is thought to constitute outreach. You will be bold and courageous while being suffused with joy and passion.

Pastors Have Accepted the Wrong Model

One of the many wrong paths the Church has taken in the last sixty years relates to outreach and evangelism. Many programs have been developed

---

[16] Ibid, March 20 page.

over the years to assist Christians in sharing their faith. Over time these programs gave way to new ones and the process evolved from going out into the community to inviting lost people to come to our services. Generally these programs focused on growing the Church through the creation of "events" which lost people might be interested in or the reshaping of the services from focusing on the believer's edification, encouragement, and equipping to focusing on the lost person. Naturally, this new focus meant reducing the amount of time spent teaching the Bible because of the belief that while lost people don't know the Bible they can relate to stories with a moral truth sprinkled in. So, many church services across America became story time with drama skits, musical performances, and other vignettes all designed to lead lost people to biblical truth in the hope they would "get it" and come to faith in Jesus Christ. Today all of these strategies fall under the general heading of Church Growth principles.

Church growth principles, whether they claim to have purpose or to be sensitive to spiritual seekers are wrong headed for a number of glaring reasons. Primarily, they are wrong because they are not biblical. Marketing and reprogramming the Church to reflect the greater culture in which it exists is simply compromise.

People who know they need God are not looking for what they can find outside the Church every day. They are looking for something that is life-changing. People who are not sure what they are seeking who also know that they do not want to continue to live as they are don't need to hear sloppy sermons about acceptance and inclusiveness.

Modern evangelism has forsaken the Gospel mission to go into the world and preach repentance for the salvation of lost sinners. Churches have decided that since Christians won't go to the lost - because it is offensive to tell people they are separated from God by their sin - they will construct events that might lure the lost into their meeting places. Churches like this will go to great lengths not to appear like a traditional church. I've even heard of churches canvassing their neighborhoods asking survey type questions such as "what would a church have to be like in order for you to attend?" Or "what do you think a church should focus on during a Sunday morning service?" This is beyond bizarre. Why in the world would Christians go ask lost people what the church should be like? Hello... McFly! Get a clue here folks.

When the Church abandons its primary evangelistic mission of Gospel proclamation it has turned its back on the greatest and most powerful resource for changed lives ever given. The Apostle Paul states it clearly: "For I am not ashamed of the gospel, for it is the power of God for salvation to everyone who believes, to the Jew first and also to the Greek." (Romans 1:16)

The household of God is exactly that – the people of God. Refashioning our meetings to lure the unsaved by making them feel accepted and welcomed is insanity. How will an unsaved person who sits under the God-anointed teaching of the Gospel feel accepted and welcomed? Have we forgotten that the work of the Holy Spirit is to bring conviction of sin? (John 16:8)

Why in the world would we want lost people who are going to hell to come and be comfortable in our times of Bible teaching, prayer, and worship? Invite people most certainly, but do not try to soften or minimize the Holy Spirit's power to save a soul trapped in sin. You are not assisting the Lord's work in the lives of your friends if you apologize for Bible teaching that raises lots of questions, worship that focuses on God, and the genuine love of the brethren displayed toward one another.

What we need today is a powerful move of the Holy Spirit upon us so that we go forth fearlessly and boldly proclaiming to this dying world that only Jesus saves.[17] We have a great cloud of witnesses surrounding us who provide powerful testimony to the power of God to save.[18] Therefore let us throw off the shackles of our age that do nothing but entangle us and prevent us from running this race of courage that God has called us into. Let us endure to the end for the glory of God and the salvation of the lost.

Shepherds you have your marching orders. Convey them to the sheep God

[17] Acts 14:3
[18] Hebrews 12:1-3

has raised you up to shepherd. Then lead them out into the cultural trenches with gladness and joy knowing that God is with you in this great mission of grace and mercy to the dead and perishing.

Chapter 4 – Get Equipped: Understand the Times Like the Men of Issachar

Of the sons of Issachar, men who understood the times, with knowledge of what Israel should do, their chiefs were two hundred; and all their kinsmen were at their command. 1 Chronicles 12:32

One of the amazing things about the Church in America today is the rampant ignorance when it comes to understanding the times in which we live. I don't say this with any gladness, but the Church in America is infantile and feebleminded when it comes to understanding what is happening in America and certainly throughout the world today.

The painful irony of this sad condition is that we live in a world that runs on a constant newsfeed. Americans walk around with mobile computers in their hands nearly every waking moment. Our children are the most technologically savvy generation to date. They feast on a smorgasbord of images, music, headlines, and entertainment. And yet, the vast majority of Americans cannot tell you who their Senator or Congressman is in Washington DC. Even worse, they don't care that they don't know.

But turn the topic to Hollywood stars, the latest Apple technology, or social media platforms that highlight their users amazing lives, and you will have an endless stream of banter about the most inane subjects imaginable. Something is clearly out of balance.

Statistics are just as troubling when we turn our attention to Christians. The manual for faith and practice, the guide book for righteous living, the one instrument in the believers arsenal that is most neglected is the Bible. How can this be? Especially given Jesus' statement as recorded by John:

> If you continue in My word, *then* you are truly disciples of Mine; and you will know the truth, and the truth will make you free. (John 8:31-32)

Discarding the Bible Results in Disaster Every Time

It would be easy to blame biblical criticism and the philosophies of modernism and postmodernism for the fall of the Bible from most read to most neglected in the Church today, but there is more to the story than just that. There has been a discernable shift in what Christians listen to, pay attention to, and base their conclusions on.

If you have made it this far dear reader then you have realized that I enjoy much of what A.W. Tozer wrote. The Church would benefit tremendously from a new generation of pastors with the spiritual insight that Tozer had. He summed up the Church's present dilemma well when he said, "The difficulty we modern Christians face is not misunderstanding the Bible, but persuading our untamed hearts to accept its plain instructions. Our problem is to get the consent of our world-loving minds to make Jesus Lord in fact as well as in word."[19]

Pastor Chuck Smith understood the times in which we live as well. He stated:

> There is a real battle for the Bible taking place in our world today. The battle isn't necessarily outside the church, between those who

---

[19] Tozer quote found here - https://www.cmalliance.org/devotions/tozer?id=1546 Accessed February 26, 2018.

don't believe in God and those in the church who do believe in God. Sadly, the battle for the Bible is found within the church, even with some pastors leading the attack against the Bible.[20]

When Christians abandon the Bible they give up their only sure anchor in a raging sea of ideas, philosophies, and today more than ever, the opinions of every man and woman that form a choke-hold of deception. How do Christians expect to navigate through life without a sure foundation of the Word?

The time in which we live today is the absolute worst time for Christians to be sleep walking through life. There is so much satanic activity assaulting our society that it becomes mind-numbing to consider it all. That is perhaps one reason why many believers have checked out. They are content to go to work, church, and out for a meal each week and then begin the process all over again each Monday. They hope they can fly under the radar of trouble by not calling any attention to themselves.

Is that what God's warriors were created for? Did God save you to enjoy your best life now? Isn't there more to this life than just living, dying and trying to make it through each day?

The reason so many believers do not engage the culture is because they neither understand what the Bible says about spiritual warfare nor do they see any connection between the Bible's many calls to action and their lives. I discuss spiritual warfare in more detail in Chapter 8. Here I want to mention just a few things that you need to know.

Satan is a deceiver and a liar, and he has been one from the beginning. Everything that he speaks is a lie. He directly contradicts truth or he distorts truth. Either way, everything he speaks is a lie. We have several choices when confronted with the lies of the evil one. We can rebuke him and them, accept the lies, or allow them to cast doubt in our minds. If the last two of these three choices are employed they will eventually lead every man or women to a devastating and tragic ending.

---

[20] A Message from Pastor Chuck Smith in Harold Lindsell, *The Battle for the Bible* (Calvary Chapel Publishing, Costa Mesa, CA 2008), p. 9.

Satan schemes constantly against you.[21] He hates all of God's creation and desires to see every soul of every man and woman destroyed. Given these facts it is incredible that Christians neglect the very manual that gives every detail of the plan of victory over Satan.

Christians simply must get back to a robust study of the Bible. It is timeless, speaking to every heart of every person if given the chance. Not only that, but the Bible speaks to every time under the sun. It is never out dated or irrelevant. That so much energy is spent by Luciferians to attack it should serve as an inspiration to Christians to cling all the more tightly to it. If the enemies of God hate it then you must know it is invaluable to believers in every age.

Then with an unshakeable assurance in God and His word, Christians must analyze the news through the filter of God's wisdom using the discernment of the Holy Spirit as a guide. There is much to discern today.

Fake News is Everywhere Today But it Has Always Existed by Another Name

The prince of the power of the air[22] is working overtime stirring up rebellion and disobedience in the hearts of people. He has waited a long time to employ his strategies that gained him the name "prince of the power of the air." He is reaching more people than ever before with his lies and demonic subterfuge and he is using technology to do it.

Satan conquered the universities decades ago. He gutted the minds of young people with cultural Marxism and the promises of a utopian wonderland. He used drugs and fornication as a sledge hammer to bludgeon the minds of the "make love not war" generation while rallying his dupes to the field with people like Timothy Leary who famously quipped "turn on, tune in, drop out" to capture his so-called anti-establishment anarchy. The legacy of the 1960's radicals is a multi-

---

[21] 2 Corinthians 2:11
[22] Ephesians 2:2

generational horde of mindless, zombie robots all marching to the same satanic drumbeat and mouthing the same incoherent nonsense that proves both Huxley and Orwell were visionaries.

Fake news is the term we give to what we used to call propaganda. It is an old scheme used for centuries to divert the attention and energy of those who fall victim to its distortions. Satan lies behind fake news and is utilizing it today with never before seen success.

We are warned of this in Ephesians 6:10-12 where Paul encourages us to:

> Finally, be strong in the Lord, and in the strength of His might. Put on the full armor of God, that you may be able to stand firm against the schemes of the devil. For our struggle is not against flesh and blood, but against the rulers, against the powers, against the world forces of this darkness, against the spiritual forces of wickedness in the heavenly places.

Take note of the following facts in this brief summary of spiritual warfare. They are imperative for every believer to understand.

- Our strength comes from the Lord. Be strong in Him.

- We are to put on all of God's armor. The implication is that we put it on and leave it on.

- When we wear the armor of God we are able to withstand Satan's schemes.

- Schemes or wiles in the KJV mean methods or methodologies. In this context it means the trickery of Satan.

- Satan has many servants in this world and he is the controlling power behind their behavior, their worldview, and their hatred of Christians.

- There is a hierarchy of demons maneuvering about in the supernatural realm.

Why is all of this important to understand? It is important to understand because when you do the chaos we see in America today – the rise of racist identity movements such as Black Lives Matter, La Raza, the New Black Panthers, and the Nation of Islam spewing forth hatred of whites and Jews, the massive invasion of illegal immigrants including those being forcibly "resettled" into unsuspecting American cities and towns, the government indoctrination centers otherwise known as the public school system that attempt to hide their Islamic indoctrination of our children, and the new orthodoxy of multiculturalism and diversity – everything begins to make sense.

The new censorship war is currently being waged against any voice, any viewpoint, or any opinion that falls outside of the accepted perspectives of the new media gestapo at YouTube, Google, Twitter, Facebook, and others. Dissent will get you banned from those platforms. Media in America has become a very useful tool in Satan's hand. They cannot be trusted and the day has arrived when believers may need to give serious consideration to abandoning these platforms completely in favor of building new ones where freedom, liberty, truth, and righteousness can prevail.

What Can Christians Do?

The new front of the spiritual war raging today is clearly information. The thinking is that if you control the flow of information you can control people. This is as old as the Garden of Eden when the Nachash whispered to Eve "Indeed, has God said?"[23]

So what must Christians do? What are some steps to take to overcome this encroaching darkness?

First, Christians must get their houses in order. What I mean by that is they

---

[23] Genesis 3:1

must stop play acting. Christians filled with the spirit of God should look like something extraordinarily different from the world today.[24] If you are walking by the power of the Holy Spirit you won't find any enjoyment in the things of the world, even the things that may have used to bring you joy. Your heart will be in tune with God's heart for your family and community.

Second, Christians must get spiritually equipped. They must put on God's armor. A Christian without God's armor is a train wreck waiting to happen, and as the saying goes it is not a matter of if but of when that train wreck occurs. If you want to comprehend the seriousness of this fight then I suggest you acquire a copy of William Gurnall's, *The Christian in Complete Armour*[25] and read it immediately. In fact this would be a great resource for a family or group study.

Third, stop listening to the mainstream media. They are liars telling lies upon lies upon lies. They all work from the same script that is carefully scrubbed clean of anything that might give people an idea that something is not right spiritually in America. There are hundreds of alternative news sources that you can find that will give you varying degrees of information that is far closer to the truth than anything the alphabet media companies are permitted to and willing to broadcast. I suggest you start with The Hagmann and Hagmann Report[26], On the Objective[27], The Common Sense Show[28], Caravan to Midnight[29], Coach Dave Live[30], Soaring Eagle Radio[31], and The Health Ranger[32]. There are many others but these will help get you started on the right path and will undoubtedly lead you to many other shows that are doing their part to provide truthful information to every man and woman who seeks it.

---

[24] Ephesians 5:3-5
[25] Wiiliam Gurnall, *The Christian in Complete Armour* (The Banner of Truth Trust, Carlisle, PA, 1989).
[26] https://www.hagmannreport.com/
[27] https://ontheobjective.org/
[28] http://www.thecommonsenseshow.com/
[29] https://www.caravantomidnight.com/
[30] https://coachdavelive.com/
[31] http://www.soaringeagleradio.com
[32] http://www.healthranger.com/

A little known fact is that about 90% of the big media in America is owned by just six major corporations.[33] If you know anything about corporations, you know that they spend millions of dollars every year to carefully craft their public image. There is no way they are going to allow the inconvenience of truth to get in the way of their profits or ideological agenda. This goal also affects their hiring practices. That is the reason the overwhelming majority of journalists walk in lock-step with the abortion industry, the LGBT industry, the cult of multiculturalism and diversity, and every other far-left idea that comes down the pike. Truth is power and so is hiding the truth. American media has sold its soul for mammon and truth is the casualty. As Dr. Ron Paul so famously quipped, "Truth is treason in the empire of lies."[34]

Because the American media is a wholly owned subsidiary of the enemies of Christ, it is imperative that Christians disconnect from them at every source. We simply cannot continue to allow our families, friends, neighbors, and co-workers to think that what they see on the daily news programs or in most of our print media is anything less than sheer propaganda. The Apostle Paul wrote to the Ephesian believers that they must guard themselves against deception. We would do well to heed this within the current context of American media.

> Let no one deceive you with empty words, for because of these things the wrath of God comes upon the sons of disobedience. Therefore do not be partakers with them; for you were formerly darkness, but now you are light in the Lord; walk as children of light for the fruit of the light consists of in all goodness and righteousness and truth trying to learn what is pleasing to the Lord. And do not participate in the unfruitful deeds of darkness, but instead even expose them;[35]

The final thing I suggest you do will be uncomfortable for a season but as the song says "joy comes in the morning." If you are attending a church in

---

[33] See https://ivn.us/2012/06/18/did-you-know-that-just-6-corporations-control-90-of-the-media-in-america-infographic/ Accessed March 10,2018.
[34] Ron Paul, *Revolution: A Manifesto* (Grand Central Publishing, New York, NY 2008).
[35] Ephesians 5:6-11

which the pastor would rather spend the precious time he has in front of God's people telling you about his vacation, the latest book he is reading, his many friends in the community, and how we simply must be nicer so that we can make the world a better place then please get out of that place as fast as you can.

The truth is that many churches in America today have become nothing more than social clubs where friends can meet a few times a week, enroll their children in what they believe are safe activities, and live the quiet life that America affords to many. If that is you dear reader then may I offend you at this point? Stop acting like life is a sitcom where everything is meant to be awesome. Stop acting like it is a birthright to not have to face tribulation and persecution. God has called His children to the war. He has instructed us to tell our children about Him and this war we are fighting. He has told us to be bold and courageous in the face of the enemy.[36] We are commanded to renew our minds in Christ day by day. That begins with you waking up to reality. Can the Church of Jesus Christ count on you?

---

[36] Joshua 1:9

Chapter 5 – Put On God's Armor: Recognize What is Available

Finally, be strong in the Lord and in the strength of His might. Put on the full armor of God, so that you will be able to stand firm against the schemes of the devil. For our struggle is not against flesh and blood, but against the rulers, against the powers, against the world forces of this darkness, against the spiritual forces of wickedness in the heavenly places. Ephesians 6:10-12

I read a story recently about a man who dreamed for years about taking a vacation on a cruise ship. He scrimped and saved everything he could so that after several years he had enough to buy the tickets. However, he also knew that he could not afford to eat his meals in the ship's restaurant and so he packed two loaves of bread and a big jar of peanut butter.

The first couple of days the man enjoyed his vacation. The sun, sea, and activities on board were fantastic but when meal time came around he began to regret that he had not been able to save more money so that he could enjoy at least a few of the wonderful foods he smelled.

It was the penultimate day of the cruise and the ship's bell rang out for the passengers to come to the dining hall for another buffet. As the man slowly left the deck to return to his room for another peanut butter sandwich another man stopped him and remarked, "Sir I have noticed that every time the meal bell rings you leave. If you don't mind me asking why do you not join us? The food is simply fantastic." The man hung his head and admitted that he only had enough money to buy the tickets. Enjoying the buffet was out of the question. With an arched brow the man's fellow traveler said, "But sir, the food for the entire cruise is included in the price of your ticket."

Many Christians are just like the man in this illustration when it comes to knowing about the vast resources at their disposal. We have been given the authority of Jesus Christ to stand against the enemy that seeks to steal, kill, and destroy everything that God has created. And yet much of modern Christendom behaves like paupers.

In the previous chapter I mentioned the armor of God and encouraged readers to make sure that you suit up and stay suited up. In this chapter I want to delve a little deeper into what this means for every believer.

In his letter to the churches of Ephesus the Apostle Paul declares to them this sobering reality: walking with Christ, proclaiming Him as Lord, and submitting yourself to Him as a servant submits to his master - includes enlistment in God's army. Paul says every Christian is a warrior in The King's army. The problem is many don't know they are part of a fighting force and therefore don't pay any attention to commands to train for the spiritual battle we are thrust into.

Consider these passages in light of the warfare we are involved in:

> Be on the alert, stand firm in the faith, act like men, be strong. (1 Corinthians 16:13)

> For though we walk in the flesh, we do not war according to the flesh, for the weapons of our warfare are not of the flesh, but divinely powerful for the destruction of fortresses. *We are* destroying speculations and every lofty thing raised up against the knowledge of God, and *we are* taking every thought captive to the obedience of Christ. (2 Corinthians 10:3-5)

The night is almost gone, and the day is near. Therefore let us lay aside the deeds of darkness and put on the armor of light. Let us behave properly as in the day, not in carousing and drunkenness, not in sexual promiscuity and sensuality, not in strife and jealousy. But put on the Lord Jesus Christ, and make no provision for the flesh in regard to *its* lusts. (Romans 13:12-14)

Then he said to me, "This is the word of the LORD to Zerubbabel saying, 'Not by might nor by power, but by My Spirit,' says the LORD of hosts. (Zechariah 4:6)

Beloved, I urge you as aliens and strangers to abstain from fleshly lusts which wage war against the soul (1 Peter 2:11)

Simon, Simon, behold, Satan has demanded *permission* to sift you like wheat; (Luke 22:31)

Beloved, do not be surprised at the fiery ordeal among you, which comes upon you for your testing, as though some strange thing were happening to you; (1 Peter 4:12)

Indeed, all who desire to live godly in Christ Jesus will be persecuted. (2 Timothy 3:12)

This only scratches the surface of what Scripture says about the ongoing battle all believers face. But back once more to my point: why are so many Christians clueless about the battle raging all around them? My belief is that the problem starts in the pulpit. Many pastors, if they speak out about the evils of our day at all, only address the symptoms. The enemy is alcohol! The enemy is pornography! The enemy is greed! This is evidenced by their proposed solutions which normally focus on programs that deal with the after-effects of addictions and sinful behavior.

Our enemy is neither flesh and blood nor any other thing in this space and time dimension we occupy. The enemy is the dragon of old and he will not be defeated by railing against alcohol. Only through the redemption Jesus

Christ offers through faith does anyone overcome anything. Every addiction, every sexual deviancy, every self-centered behavior that destroys us physically, emotionally, and spiritually finds it root in the father of lies. (John 8:44)

The Bible says that God's people perish due to a lack of knowledge.[37] In context God calls out Israel for their unfaithfulness. They were to be a light to the nations and a model of what God's righteousness looks like in a people who love Him and pursue His ways. They missed the boat on all of that.

I believe God is calling out America's churches in large measure because they have been unfaithful. Some may be offended at that statement and ask defiantly how they have been spiritually adulterous? Listen to God's criticism of Israel through the prophet Hosea and see if any of it applies.

> Listen to the word of the LORD, O sons of Israel,
> For the LORD has a case against the inhabitants of the land,
> Because there is no faithfulness or kindness
> Or knowledge of God in the land.
> *There is* swearing, deception, murder, stealing and adultery.
> They employ violence, so that bloodshed follows bloodshed.
> Therefore the land mourns,
> and everyone who lives in it languishes.
> (Hosea 4:1-3a)

Increasingly in America there is no knowledge of God in the land. I will speak to this at length in Chapter 11. For now please understand that without knowledge of God, His truth, His precepts, and His principles, there will be no overcoming of anything that American's suffer. Oppression will continue and no amount of tax dollars authorized for new programs will ever achieve their goal.

How do we overcome in this war we are in? How do we manage to outflank, out maneuver, and outsmart the enemy? It starts by recognizing our strength in Christ. Paul wrote to the Ephesians to "be strong in the Lord and in the strength of His might." What does that mean? That means

---

[37] Hosea 4:6

we must recognize that Christ defeated Satan at the cross and because we are in Christ by faith and Christ is in us, we have defeated Satan as well. Depend on Christ's strength that is yours st every moment. Recognize what is yours spiritually.

Then notice that we are to do something else, something more. We are to put on the full armor of God. Put it all on, not just some of it. The entire suit of armor is available, so why would you leave something off and create a vulnerability for the enemy to exploit?

Take note of whose armor it is. It is God's armor. God outfits you for the battles you face with His provision. God is our field commander, our Supreme General and He says that we will need His provision in Christ to stand firm against the enemy's strategies.

This will come as a surprise to some reading this book, but God's enemy, the Nachash, the serpent of old, the great dragon, seeks to destroy God's people. When was the last time you considered that you are on Satan's hit list? Sobering thought isn't it? Since that is true the importance of suiting up with God's armor every day should be of the utmost importance.

The Battle-Ready Believer

I enjoy recommending books to other believers for their edification and encouragement. One that I have benefitted from personally is *The Battle-Ready Believer* written by Michael Boldea Jr. In his book Michael lays out a complete battle plan, covering enlistment, basic training, familiarity with standard issue weapons, proficiency in the use of these weapons, learning to follow orders from our General, recognizing the enemy, and understanding the ultimate goal of our service to our King. It reads like a modern day manual for spiritual warfare. Concerning our weapons Michael writes:

> When it comes to weapons, there are weapons of defense, weapons of attack, and weapons that in a pinch can pull double duty and be used both for attack as well as for defense. The believer's arsenal of weapons is clearly itemized within God's Word, and this is done so

we can go through the checklist, inventory our gear, see if anything is missing, and if we are, in fact, ready for battle.

Although the notion of preparedness has fallen out of favor in recent times, like so many other practical and necessary virtues, one understands the true importance of preparedness only when it's too late.

If I only realize my shield and blade are rusty when I take my stand on the battlefield, it is likely too late to do anything about it. If we do not do our utmost to prepare for the eventuality of battle, even before the battle begins the enemy has a distinct advantage due to our failure to assign the correct level of importance to the task of preparation, making sure our armor and our weapons are as they ought to be.[38]

Let me suggest a new approach to Bible study. Consider that every time you sit down either alone or in a group setting to study the Bible, you are actually called into a strategy conference with God, your Commanding General, to go over the battle plans for the day. One of the many questions the Commanding General is going to ask is this: do you have adequate provisions to engage the enemy at the designated point of attack?

Here is what is available to you Christian:

> Stand firm therefore, HAVING GIRDED YOUR LOINS WITH TRUTH, and HAVING PUT ON THE BREASTPLATE OF RIGHTEOUSNESS, and having shod YOUR FEET WITH THE PREPARATION OF THE GOSPEL OF PEACE; in addition to all, taking up the shield of faith with which you will be able to extinguish all the flaming arrows of the evil *one*. And take THE HELMET OF SALVATION, and the sword of the Spirit, which is the word of God. With all prayer and petition pray at all times in the Spirit, and with this in view, be on the alert with all perseverance and petition for all the saints. (Ephesians 6:14-18)

---

[38] Michael Boldea Jr., *The Battle-Ready Believer* (Boldman Publishing, Watertown, WI, 2016), p. 118.

Do you see your provisions? Do you see those weapons of warfare that each believer is issued upon entrance into the Kingdom of God through faith? Here's the list:

- Truth
- Breastplate of Righteousness
- Gospel of Peace
- Shield of Faith
- Helmet of Salvation
- Sword of the Spirit
- Prayer
- Alertness
- Perseverance

Paul used the imagery of a Roman soldier and his gear to express several significant spiritual truths in his letter to the Ephesian believers. He starts with "girding your loins with truth." Other translations use similar words but the idea is to strap on truth like you do a belt. It is significant that it is the first piece of God's armor that we are to put on.

What is truth? It is whatever God says it is. God Himself is truth itself. Truth is in short supply today. Given this reality, the Church should be portioning out truth by the truckload. Instead it is sounding a steady drumbeat of retreat from the culture wars and every other area where conflict might arise. Don't worry be happy seems to be the mission statement of far too many churches and their congregants.

The truth is that God created man and said that it was not good for man to be alone, so God created woman as well as the covenant of marriage between a man and a woman. That is truth. God created them male and female. That is truth too. God created one race and named it mankind. Therefore, racism is a lie and so is the greatest support system for racism Satan has ever whispered into man's ear: the theory of evolution. I could go on and on but I think you get the point. Truth is what God says it is. If your "reality" is opposed to God's reality then you are in open rebellion. You cannot walk with God and deny His truth. Indeed knowing truth will set you free[39] from the chains of deception that Satan has shackled all people in who remain apart from Christ,[40] and those who profess Christ but have succumbed to his lies.

The breastplate of righteousness is the righteousness of Jesus Christ imputed to us through faith in Christ's finished work on Calvary's Cross.[41] The breastplate protected the vital organs, most notably the heart, of the Roman soldier... A sword or spear thrust to the heart was fatal. The application for the believer is that Christ's righteousness protects our hearts and indeed allows for growth in understanding, righteousness, and holiness. The enemy would like nothing more than to steal your joy, peace, and assurance because then the heart for Christ, the heart that hungers and thirsts for righteousness,[42] while seeking to obey Him, will grow callous and careless in the things it entertains. The flame of passion for Christ will grow dimmer such that He will inquire of them "where is that love with which you first loved Me?"[43]

The Gospel of peace is the next item in our spiritual armor. This is especially needed today in our world filled with anxious and worried people in addition to a plethora of medications aimed at bringing balance and stability to weary lives. This component of equipment in our armor is actually quite exciting. It says that this Gospel which we proclaim and by which we have been saved will bring true peace to all those who embrace its truths. In other words the peace that seems so hard to acquire and harder still to hang on to for many millions in America today is a free gift from God through faith in Jesus Christ. When people are born-again by faith they are finally at peace with God. The Bible says that Jesus has removed the enmity between God and man.[44] That means there is peace with God and that Jesus is the peace of God in us. How beautiful are the feet of those who bring this message to a sick and starving soul?

---

[39]John 8:31-32
[40]2 Corinthians 4:4
[41] 2 Corinthians 5:21
[42] Matthew 5:6
[43] Revelation 2:4
[44] Ephesians 2:15-16

The shield of faith is our protection against the fiery darts of our enemy. Faith extinguishes the lies of Satan, stops his schemes from harming us and others, illuminates the path forward out of every hill and vale, and is our strength to cling to Christ regardless of our circumstances. Great is His faithfulness toward us friends, and knowing this energizes us to finish our course for His glory and honor. Faith in faith is a lie but faith in the faithful One will equip you to prevail.

The helmet of salvation is a most precious gift and one that the enemy tries to dislodge with ferocity. The helmet of salvation is our assurance of God's promises fulfilled in Christ. Sowing doubt is an effective strategy of our enemy. He does this routinely through relationships, circumstances, and even world events. This piece of armor is so important that the Apostle Paul said to the Roman believers that we must transform our minds[45] so that we do not allow worldly ideas, opinions, and the anxiety over either to enter in. Instead we are to guard our minds so that our lives demonstrate that His promises are true and to focus on that which is good and acceptable and perfect. This in turn allows us to remember day by day that God has freed us from the penalty of sin. We are indeed dead to sin and alive to God in Jesus Christ.[46]

The next piece of God's armor is a most powerful weapon that we can and must use both defensively and offensively. The Sword of the Spirit is the Bible. Can you imagine a dusty, rusty, and dull sword being wielded to any positive effect in battle? Me neither. The soldier that would dare treat his best defensive and offensive weapon in such a fashion is clearly derelict in duty and would not fare well on the battlefield.

The importance of the Word of God for our daily living was demonstrated in the clearest possible fashion by Jesus Himself. After His baptism He was immediately led into the surrounding wilderness where Satan tried to cause Jesus to worship him. Three attempts were made by the evil one and three times Christ responded with "It is written," showing the significance of the Word of God in our battle against the forces of darkness. This is why Scripture memorization is a valuable discipline. Having the Word of God

---

[45] Romans 12:1-2
[46] Romans 6:11

available when you meet difficult situations equips you to meet them with confidence.

The final three things in our arsenal are devoted to making sure that the previous weapons are utilized and maintained in a state of readiness. We are to be devoted to prayer at all times. This keeps us sensitive to the Holy Spirit and alerts us when trouble is ahead. We are to persevere in this state of readiness as a good soldier of Christ. This is what it means to stand firm against the schemes of the enemy.

Recognize friends that our enemy and his cohorts ultimately reside in the supernatural realm while attempting to influence us in space and time. They utilize every form of wickedness known to them to try and destroy us. Call upon your heavenly Father day by day for all you need in this battle. God gives you all you need to fight this fight until Christ returns. He is all inclusive in His free gift of salvation. It is up to you to open your eyes and ears to see and hear. Once you know the truth and have been set free, run to the front of the battle.

Chapter 6 – Appeal to Your Local Magistrates: Holding Civil Authorities Accountable

When they had brought them, they stood them before the Council. The high priest questioned them, saying, "We gave you strict orders not to continue teaching in this name, and yet, you have filled Jerusalem with your teaching and intend to bring this man's blood upon us." But Peter and the apostles answered, "We must obey God rather than men.
Acts 5:27-29

One of the primary assaults upon Christianity in America has been the Federal Government. In its quest to create its notion of an egalitarian, utopian dream it has socially engineered a nightmare for liberty and freedom minded people, most especially for citizens who also happen to be born again believers in the Lord Jesus Christ. In doing this, the Federal Government has overstepped its authority and has become a tyranny of anti-God spewing hatred and bigotry toward true biblical Christianity.

I make a distinction above between true biblical Christianity and Christianity in name only. In reality there is a significant number of people who claim to be followers of Jesus Christ who have no issues with the Federal Government's overreach and who unflinchingly believe in total submission to the government at every level. For these people Romans 13 is the proof text that demonstrates that Christians should submit to whatever authority happens to be in power at the time.

But is that actually true? Can believers appeal to Romans 13 or any other passage of Scripture as the reason why Christians should remain silent on a variety of issues affecting them? I do not believe that Romans 13 teaches anything remotely close to what the Church in general has taught for decades.

A Brief Consideration of Romans 13:1-5[47]

Noah Webster had much to say about the role of government and the responsibility of citizens to administer such government. For example Webster stated:

- "If the citizens neglect their duty and place unprincipled men in office, the government will soon be corrupted; laws will be made not for the public good so much as for selfish or local purposes."

- "If the government fails to secure public prosperity and happiness, it must be because the citizens neglect the Divine Commands, and elect bad men to make and administer the Law."

- "The Bible must be considered as the great source of all the truth by which men are to be guided in government as well as in all government transactions."

When you begin speaking about the role of government, American Christians almost universally state that people are to obey the government unequivocally, with only minor exceptions such as when it might attempt to make you do something that directly contradicts God's commands. They

---

[47] This edited version of "A Brief Consideration of Romans 13" appeared originally as an article on http://www.thetransformingword.com/?p=81

don't really believe that at all. They merely say that in order to continue to live their lives without any cognitive dissonance.

The Romans 13 passage actually has much to say about the authority, function, and place of government that many Christians simply do not understand because either they've never heard it preached correctly or they've never studied the passage for themselves. I have heard people say that they are not voting because the system is rigged anyway - a belief I share - and still others say that it doesn't matter who you vote for because they are all the same - again I agree with that perspective. A precious few get to the heart of the matter by saying that the current government America has in place is not described in Romans 13 but is described elsewhere by the phrase "spirit of antichrist."

Let's jump into a brief survey. How many times have you heard a Christian say, "God put the President in office so it is our duty to obey him"? I hear that a lot, but is it really true? The only passage in the New Testament that someone who holds this view can point to is Romans 13, but in my opinion this passage says nothing of the sort concerning who gets elected to what office. Romans 13 is not concerned about that in the least.

Please take the time to read Romans 13:1-5 now before you continue reading.

If as some Christians say, "God puts people in office and it is our duty to respect and honor them" then it follows that God has placed every despot, tyrant, murderer, and psychopath throughout history in office and it is our duty to honor and respect them. There is a Greek word that is used for this mental disease of uncritical and unbiblical thinking: baloney. This conclusion implies that God purposefully placed Hitler, the Ayatollahs of Islam, Mao, Stalin, and every murdering psychopath who has rested power from their people into positions where they committed heinous acts of evil against innocent people.

Some people try to use a couple of Old Testament passages including 1 Chronicles 28:4 where David says, "The Lord, the God of Israel chose me from all the house of my father to be King over Israel forever." Daniel 2:21 is another verse that people sometimes point to: "It is He who changes the times and the epochs; He removes Kings and establishes Kings;" to prove that God establishes each individual in a position of authority.

Are these passages teaching as doctrine that God raises up leaders and puts them in place and therefore validates the common Romans 13 understanding? Not at all. Theses scriptures are anecdotal in nature and show that God was involved in raising up Israel's Kings and sometimes those of her neighbors. No doctrine can be derived from these examples.

Are there any New Testament examples to support the common understanding of Romans 13? No. Not even one. We cannot say biblically, "well God raised up this President or these nine Supreme Court Justices, or these Senators, etc., so we must obey them."

The New Testament introduces us to the doctrine of grace and free will. We do not live in a theocracy. This is no truer than when we are exercising our freedoms to vote and to affect public policy in favor of righteousness to the extent that is possible.

We as a people can choose to make God-honoring decisions concerning public policy and elect God-honoring people to office. As recent decades clearly demonstrate, the opposite is also true.

When we make God-dishonoring decisions we end up with God-dishonoring leaders and laws. We can't say "God put the nine Supreme Court justices in place who forced sodomite marriage upon America so we'll just have to live with it." God didn't do that. We the people did that through the Presidents and representatives we elected to office.

Now how does all this relate to Romans 13? Note verse 1 in which God establishes order in His creation by establishing government. Government is nothing more than the framework by which people govern themselves. It is a mutually agreed upon pact among the people of a nation who establish rules that structure their relationship to one another.

God does not dictate democracy, socialism, or any other manmade system of political theory. He merely states there should be order concerning nations in order to sustain human life and society. There are three interesting words used in this passage: subjection – verse 1 and 5, resists – verse 2 , and ordinance – verse 2.

All three of these words have the same root in the Greek: *taso*. *Taso* means "to appoint."

- Subjection is *hupo-taso*. We get the prefix hyper from this word; hypodermic for example means under the skin. Subjection means to be <u>under</u> authority.

- Resist is *anti-taso*; meaning against the appointment or authority.

- Ordinance is *dia-taso*. This word means thorough or complete. Think of diagnosis, which means thorough knowledge. Therefore, that which is ordained is something that is thoroughly appointed.

How does all this fit together? We are to be *hupo-taso*, subject to, and not *anti-taso*, opposed to, that which God has *dia-taso*, ordained. What has God ordained? God has ordained government as an abstract and necessary structure of order, nothing else.

Now let's look at the most overlooked part of this entire passage, the qualifiers.

- Verse 1: Every soul is to be in subjection to the governing authority of God. There is no authority but from God. In other words, God establishes governments to represent Him, and to exercise authority based on His character.

- Verse 2: "Therefore," because God has ordained that mankind live an orderly life under His authority, those who resist God's authority when rightly present will receive condemnation.

Our mandate is crystal clear here. Must we obey whatever government is over you? No! We must obey governments that demonstrate God-honoring laws and conduct toward their citizens. Verses 3 and 4 provide further clarification on what authority must look like if Romans 13 is to apply.

- Verse 3: "For," or because, properly functioning, God-ordained authority rewards good, Godly behavior, good insofar as it lines up with what God calls good.

- In other words, God-ordained authority rewards God-honoring people and punishes evil, God-dishonoring behavior.

- Verse 4: "For," or because God ordained authority is meant to be a minister to equip citizens to lead a God-honoring life while recognizing that because of free will many will choose not to do so.

- For those who resist, *anti-taso*, God's authority rightly wielded by God-honoring governments, the sword is justified.

Ultimately, God does ordain government as a role to manage order, but He does not ordain specific individuals or even forms of government. Thus, God does not require submission to governments that have left their God-honoring moorings and have turned evil into good and good into evil.

For governments to operate as God's ministers, and to be identified as God-ordained, they must function as they were designed to function. When they do not they have shown that they are not entitled to receive Godly submission. Therefore, God did not establish Hitler, the German people did that. To say that God ordains covenant breakers, liars, murderers, and all forms of evil perpetrated by governments is to make God unworthy to judge the world.

If man's laws are evil and ordained by God, how can God's holy nature be reconciled with the expansive sins of unholy worldly authority? If government is truly a minister of God, then it will act like a minister of God, reflecting His character in all things.

Friends, the prevailing interpretation of Romans 13 is clearly wrong based on a study of the text. Tyrants love it when Christians resign themselves to supporting evil conduct.

Don't be deceived folks. The prevailing interpretation of Romans 13 within the majority of the Church is simply wrong.[48]

---

[48] The best treatment of this passage that I have found is James M. Wilson, "Civil Government: An Exposition of Romans 13:1-5" found at

Now with that major obstacle addressed, we need to understand what it means to make an appeal to our local authorities for right conduct involving legislation passed either by the Federal Government or local authorities. It is our duty and privilege to have this responsibility within our Constitutional republic.

Appealing to Local Magistrates[49]

Interacting proactively with government is a foreign idea to most Americans today. This is certainly proof that the Federal Government's tentacles have strangled the life out of its citizens such that most have become programmed zombies of obedience. The issue is that individual States and local governing authorities have consistently capitulated to the demands of the Federal Government. They do so with the excuse that they have no choice because whatever the Federal Government says is the law of the land.

Let's take the recent abomination of a demand from the Federal Government that government schools, public is a misguided euphemism, allow girls and boys to utilize the same restrooms and shower facilities. Right here in Lima, Ohio, we had a school board that stated in a public meeting that they had no choice but to comply because if they did not they would not receive a significant amount of Federal funding.

I believe that this was a moment of unintended candor. The school board had every right and responsibility to tell the Federal Government that they would not comply with this evil demand. The real issue for the school board was the subsequent withholding of money. This common strategy of enforcing compliance by threatening financial deprivation has been deployed to great effect by both the Federal and State Governments.

The word magistrate refers to anyone in civil government with authority.

---

http://www.thirdmill.org/newfiles/jam_wilson/jam_wilson.CivilGovernment.pdf I also want to thank Dr. Randy White for his sermon on the same passage. His analysis of the Greek grammar and teaching on this subject is appreciated.

[49] To understand how far Christians have allowed things to get out of control I recommend a book by Matthew Trewhella, "The Doctrine of the Lesser Magistrates," found at https://lessermagistrate.com/the-man-behind-the-mission/

This includes both elected and appointed individuals. The local magistrates are your local judges, mayor, city council members, law enforcement officers, and State Government officials such as State Senators and House members who represent your district.

The responsibility of these local magistrates is to push back on any higher authority that issues an evil, tyrannical, or otherwise harmful ruling that attempts to force compliance upon everyone. The Founding Fathers were right to separate powers into branches and to hold States' rights as sovereign over the Federal Government, but today this idea has returned to being deemed revolutionary.

It is necessary today for local governing authorities to push back on evil laws that are contrary both to our Constitution and to God's design for governing. This idea is biblical and is known as interposition. God is looking for people to interpose and, to stand in the gap against evil today.[50]

When local magistrates refuse to do their job, it is the responsibility of the people to demand that they do. One case in point is the recent jailing of county clerk Kim Davis for refusing to issue same sex marriage licenses.

Besides the obvious point that two men or two women cohabitating together does not constitute a marriage, because the parameters of what a marriage is have been established by God, Davis was standing on solid ground and was interposing before an unjust judicial ruling.

She carried her conviction all the way to jail. Thankfully, thousands of Christians rose up and demanded she be released. Many hundreds if not thousands actually traveled to Kentucky to stand outside of the judge's house who sentenced Davis to jail and demanded he repent of his wickedness. This is interposition friends. Davis was ultimately released because she had not broken any law. She had, in fact, upheld the law on the books of the state of Kentucky declaring marriage to be between one man and one woman. Ironically, she would have broken the law had she actually signed the certificate that she was jailed for refusing to sign.

---

[50] See Ezekiel 22:27-31 for an example of God seeking those who would stand in the gap against government and societal evil.

Most Americans have forgotten if they ever knew in the first place, that courts do not make laws. Therefore any court including the Supreme Court of the United States does not make law and their pontificating to the contrary does not change that fact. Constitutional power to make law belongs to the legislative branch.

America has for the most part become a nation of idol worshippers. We worship ourselves, our material possessions, our leisure time, and our convoluted view of freedom. We have become blind and boastful and do not realize we have willingly become slaves.

Aldous Huxley had it right when he said in "Brave New World" that:

> A really efficient totalitarian state would be one in which the all-powerful executive of political bosses and their army of managers control a population of slaves who do not have to be coerced, because they love their servitude.[51]

Friends, America is doomed unless the Church rises up. The Church will not rise up unless Christians rise up and demand that pastors either kneel before God or get out of the way. The time for playing patty-cake with the culture is over.

---

[51] Aldous Huxley, *Brave New World* (Garden City, NY: International Collectors Library, 1946) Foreword xiii.

Chapter 7 - Organize With Other Like-Minded Believers: The Lone Ranger Was a Fictional Character

So then you are no longer strangers and aliens, but you are fellow citizens with the saints, and are of God's household, having been built on the foundation of the apostles and prophets, Christ Jesus Himself being the corner stone, in whom the whole building, being fitted together, is growing into a holy temple in the Lord, in whom you also are being built together into a dwelling of God in the Spirit. Ephesians 2:19-22

So then, those who had received his word were baptized; and that day there were added about three thousand souls. They were continually devoting themselves to the apostles' teaching and to fellowship, to the breaking of bread and to prayer. Everyone kept feeling a sense of awe; and many wonders and signs were taking place through the apostles. And all those who had believed were together and had all things in common; and they began selling their property and possessions and were sharing them with all, as anyone might have need. Day by day continuing with one mind in the temple, and breaking bread from house to house, they were taking their meals together with gladness and sincerity of heart, praising God and having favor with all the people. And the Lord was adding to their number day by day those who were being saved. Acts 2:41-47

Christians are meant to live in community with other believers in the Lord Jesus Christ. Being the body of Christ means being part of a community of believers that meets face to face on a regular basis for teaching, equipping, encouragement, edification, correction, and honoring God with our lives.

Sadly, the Church in many instances has become a grotesque mutation of the body of Christ. Splintered and badly crippled, many churches hobble along not knowing that their existence could and should be different. Consider what Jesus taught about His body.

The growth it will experience by outreach to believers and unbelievers alike:

And Jesus came and said to them, "All authority in heaven and on earth has been given to me. Go therefore and make disciples of all nations, baptizing them in the name of the Father and of the Son and of the Holy Spirit, teaching them to observe all that I have commanded you. And behold, I am with you always, to the end of the age. (Matthew 28:18-20)

The authority it will have over the enemy of God:

And I tell you, you are Peter, and on this rock I will build my church, and the gates of hell shall not prevail against it. (Matthew 16:18)

The source of its power for everything it is called to do:

but you will receive power when the Holy Spirit has come upon you; and you shall be My witnesses both in Jerusalem, and in all Judea and Samaria, and even to the remotest part of the earth. (Acts 1:8)

The exclusivity of its membership:

Enter through the narrow gate; for the gate is wide and the way is broad that leads to destruction, and there are many who enter through it. For the gate is small and the way is narrow that leads to life, and there are few who find it. (Matthew 7:13-14)

Not everyone who says to Me, 'Lord, Lord,' will enter the kingdom of heaven, but he who does the will of My Father who is in heaven *will enter.* Many will say to Me on that day, 'Lord, Lord, did we not prophesy in Your name, and in Your name cast out demons, and in Your name perform many miracles?' And then I will declare to them, 'I never knew you; DEPART FROM ME, YOU WHO PRACTICE LAWLESSNESS.' (Matthew 7:21-23)

The rest it will receive through a posture of humility before Christ:

Come to Me, all who are weary and heavy-laden, and I will give you rest. Take My yoke upon you and learn from Me, for I am gentle and humble in heart, and YOU WILL FIND REST FOR YOUR SOULS. For My yoke is easy and My burden is light. (Matthew 11:28-30)

The prayers of the Son of God that will be fulfilled in His body:

But now I come to You; and these things I speak in the world so that they may have My joy made full in themselves. I have given them Your word; and the world has hated them, because they are not of the world, even as I am not of the world. I do not ask You to take them out of the world, but to keep them from the evil *one.* They are not of the world, even as I am not of the world. Sanctify them in the truth; Your word is truth. As You sent Me into the world, I also have sent them into the world. For their sakes I sanctify Myself, that they themselves also may be sanctified in truth. "I do not ask on behalf of these alone, but for those also who believe in Me through their word; that they may all be one; even as You, Father, *are* in Me and I in You, that they also may be in Us, so that the world may believe that You sent Me. (John 17:13-21)

There is much more that Jesus said about His body but the references above present a common picture of what Jesus taught and thought about His followers and the fellowship of believers we call the Church. From this concise list of passages we see that:

- The early church focused nearly exclusively on hearing Jesus' words taught, sharing their lives together as a community, eating together, the Lord's Table, and prayer.
- Signs and wonders accompanied their preaching.
- They supported each other and helped to meet everyone's needs as they arose.
- That His body would be Holy Spirit powered in all it does.
- That the enemy would never prevail against it.
- False conversions would be frequent, and that only those who humble themselves before God will be saved. Those who are born again are the true members of the body.
- Not everyone who claims to be a Christian is actually one.
- The sanctification of the body is in and through Christ. It is a work of grace.

An unavoidable truth is that the Church is a body of believers who meet together regularly and share their lives together for the glory of God. All manner of ministry comes from this common union we have in Christ. Some of you might be wondering why I am laboring this point. I am emphasizing this point of community because today the Church is being attacked as irrelevant, outdated, carnal, and unnecessary. James Bannerman has a word for people who think this way. He said, "Without the existence of a Church, or of a body of believers, as contradistinguished from believers individually, very much of what is contained in the Bible would be unintelligible, and without practical application."[52]

Here's a newsflash for people that believe the Church is dead: it cannot die!

---

[52] Bannerman was a Scottish theologian and pastor best known for his classic work on Presbyterian ecclesiology, *The Church of Christ.*

Jesus has given all believers His Spirit (Romans 8:9) and nothing in this world or the supernatural realm can overcome the called-out ones of God. If you oppose the Church you have set yourself against Jesus. I know that statement ruffles some feathers. I have a one word reply: Good! There are many people that need a word of correction on the subject of the Church.

There's a saying we use all the time when trying to bring a gentle word of correction to people: don't throw the baby out with the bathwater. Friend, there certainly are many churches that are not of Christ. Those that trumpet their "inclusiveness," their "diversity," and their "progressiveness," are prime examples of wanton disregard for Jesus Christ and the Bible. As you know those are code words for "we have acquiesced to the depravity of the times." Jesus said that if you love Him you will obey His commands. It is not obedience to Jesus that fuels the rise of rebellion in the pulpits of America and consequently in many churches. It is instead the spirit of antichrist.

What Can Christians Do?

Given these challenges, what should the faithful remnant do? We should organize with like-minded believers as a first priority. I live in Ohio within driving distance of several major metropolitan areas and so making connections with other believers is easy. You may live in a more rural area where like-minded believers are few and far between. If that is the case then I suggest that you prayerfully consider starting a home Bible study and inviting others to come. It may start with only your family. Allow God to direct the effort.

I suggest that you contact as many organizations of like-minded believers as you can and ask if there are believers who live in your area. This may enable you to get a local Bible study going rather quickly. You should also check for online Bible studies from vetted churches. It is becoming more common today for churches to broadcast their services online and to upload them to various media platforms for later viewing. The church I am privileged to pastor broadcasts all our services live on the internet, uploads videos of the sermons to YouTube, and archives the audio messages on our websites. But again, even – and perhaps especially – when engaging in ministry online it is imperative to take time to learn more about the church you are being spiritually fed by.

What the remnant must also do is get educated biblically. Much of the Church has been fed information under the banner of Bible teaching that simply is not accurate. I adopted a statement several years ago that I use quite often: it is not my job to protect you from your Bible.[53]

In other words the Bible speaks directly and clearly about most things but pastors have a tendency to fall into these varieties of common errors: skirting any teaching that appears controversial, focusing on pet subjects to the exclusion of more important matters, teaching their denominational beliefs over what the Bible actual says, and, refusing to take a bold stand on moral issues that the culture has co-opted as "rights" and "justice" matters.

The body of Jesus Christ is meant to be a force to bring Gospel light to the darkness of our culture. We do that by unflinchingly proclaiming that there is salvation in no one but Jesus Christ, that God calls all people everywhere to repent of their sin and turn from their wicked ways, that Jesus Christ will return one day and He is returning as a judge, and that heaven and hell are real places.

Please take courage friends. God has promised never leave us nor forsake us and that even applies to our fellowship and labor in the fields of harvest. Prayerfully seek Him and His direction for how to get connected today.

---

[53] Hat tip to Dr. Mike Heiser.

Chapter 8 – Engage the Enemy: Strategic Warfare

Be of sober spirit, be on the alert. Your adversary, the devil, prowls around like a roaring lion, seeking someone to devour. 1 Peter 5:8

We are at war. No I'm not talking about the Military Industrial Complex's insatiable hunger for profiteering at the expense of American men and women's lives. I'm not talking about the escalating conflict between the various political factions and their comic stooges playing out in the news cycle day after day. I'm not even talking about the globalists and their open borders agenda for the destruction of national sovereignty. I'm talking about a much more devastating war with eternal consequences. The war between the fallen ones and our great God that is raging all around us.

This war has a goal. Satan and his followers seek to capture every soul that God has created for the purpose of dragging those lost ones into the pits of hell. God on the other hand is seeking to save that which is lost namely every man and woman born in Adam who remains unborn in Christ. The consequences are indeed for eternity.

The enemy is shrewd and often uses sublime tactics to deceive and divert. Alcohol, drugs, pornography, materialism, and ego are all fueled in America by abundant access to the addiction of choice.

What Does it Mean to be A Soldier of the Lord Jesus Christ?

As I mentioned earlier Christians are soldiers in the Army of God. This call on our lives is unambiguously stated in scripture:

> You therefore, my son, be strong in the grace that is in Christ Jesus. The things which you have heard from me in the presence of many witnesses, entrust these to faithful men who will be able to teach others also. Suffer hardship with *me*, as a good soldier of Christ Jesus. No soldier in active service entangles himself in the affairs of everyday life, so that he may please the one who enlisted him as a soldier. (2 Timothy 2:1-4)

A key point in that passage is this: disciples of Jesus are soldiers by birth, and the duty of every soldier is to obey their commander. Did you notice the context for this emphasized obedience? It is our desire to "please" Jesus in our every action.

Here is an important fact that all Christians must come to terms with: soldiers in God's Army are not pacifists. We are called to be "boots on the ground" people, to borrow a military phrase.

Here is a second fact that many Christians ignore: intel is vital to an army's success. What intel do we need? For starters we need intel about:

- The enemy's troop size.
- The enemy's troop movements.
- The enemy's strategies.
- The enemy's weaknesses.
- The best strategies to defeat the enemy.

Many Christians don't understand the importance of garnering intel about the enemies of God. As a consequence, they fall prey to cognitive dissonance by avoiding intel that is upsetting. Therefore a significant number of pastors muddle along determined not to upset the sheep and make it their goal to only lead them to graze in pastures of the sheep's choosing. Talk about a recipe for disaster! Letting the sheep dictate the direction of the Church creates a false sense of security for the sheep and is tantamount to allowing them to drink from polluted streams.

Refusing to understand the times in which we live has led the Church into a swampland of confusing responses and an increased level of timidity when a bold biblical response is needed. False intel is a lot like cotton candy. It dissolves quickly, is wonderfully sweet, and goes down easy. In other words it is not hard to chew, swallow, or digest. The problem is it will rot your teeth, elevate your blood sugars to dangerous levels, and provides absolutely no nourishment.

Far too much of the Church accepts false intel because it makes them comfortable and happy, but that is deception. The deception allows for comfortable and happy sheep to return week after week for more and more cotton candy and they bring their checkbooks with them. All seems well in Wonderland.

But as Lewis Carroll so famously wrote there comes a time to talk of other things:

> The time has come,' the Walrus said,
> To talk of many things:
> Of shoes — and ships — and sealing-wax —
> Of cabbages — and kings —
> And why the sea is boiling hot —
> And whether pigs have wings.'[54]

If you know anything about this poem and its meaning then you understand that the walrus and the carpenter lured a bed of oysters to their demise by talking of grand things, all intentionally misleading.

Much of the church today has been lured to the sidelines by talk of shoes and ships and sealing wax, of cabbages and kings. The walrus and the carpenter are apt descriptions of many pastors today. How many are willing to concede that thousands of pulpits are sources of fake intel? If you cannot identify the problem, then you'll never come up with a solution that works.

---

[54]This poem was recited by Carroll's characters Tweedledee and Tweedeldum in his 1871 book *Through the Looking Glass*.

What is false intel? It is not just refusing to tell the truth about America and the forces of evil that are hurling us headlong into massive social conflict. It includes the false Gospel of the "don't worry be happy" Gospel hucksters, the "have your best life now" charlatans, and the "we're all little gods" blasphemers. This kind of rotten false teaching is preached in many a pulpit week by week to a starving church. Little do these poor people understand that they are starving to death spiritually.

Seeking after and acquiring the best the world has to offer is no sign of God's favor or success. The modern day Gospel hucksters preach wealth as a birthright of "The King's Kids." The Apostle Paul says this type of person has a depraved mind and is deprived of the truth.

> If anyone advocates a different doctrine and does not agree with sound words, those of our Lord Jesus Christ, and with the doctrine conforming to godliness, he is conceited *and* understands nothing; but he has a morbid interest in controversial questions and disputes about words, out of which arise envy, strife, abusive language, evil suspicions, and constant friction between men of depraved mind and deprived of the truth, who suppose that godliness is a means of gain. But godliness *actually* is a means of great gain when accompanied by contentment. For we have brought nothing into the world, so we cannot take anything out of it either. If we have food and covering, with these we shall be content. But those who want to get rich fall into temptation and a snare and many foolish and harmful desires which plunge men into ruin and destruction. For the love of money is a root of all sorts of evil, and some by longing for it have wandered away from the faith and pierced themselves with many griefs. (1 Timothy 6:3-10)

Listen friends, if your pastor's calling is more in line with that of a motivational speaker than a fearless soldier of Christ, please get out of that place and find a real God-centered family of believers where you can grow and live a faithful action-centered life of Gospel proclamation.

If your pastor will not publically stand for Christ and denounce sin and warn of coming judgment then get out of that place and find a new body of Christ that is being faithful.

The enemy's troops have already mobilized all across America. Yet week after week hundreds of thousands of Christians go to their holy huddle and never hear a word about the evil that has America in a choke hold. The enemy is using our education system, government systems, civic organizations, and other centers of power to push for a complete and total victory of evil over good.

The true soldier of Jesus Christ does not accept the fake Christianity that renders the faith a powerless and tragic meme. The true soldier will fight the good fight to the last breath because the eternity of the lost hangs in the balance.

The Soldier's Mission

In 2 Corinthians 10:3-6 we read Paul describing some of the power of the soldier of Christ.

> For though we walk in the flesh, we do not war according to the flesh, for the weapons of our warfare are not of the flesh, but divinely powerful for the destruction of fortresses. *We are* destroying speculations and every lofty thing raised up against the knowledge of God, and *we are* taking every thought captive to the obedience of Christ, and we are ready to punish all disobedience, whenever your obedience is complete.

How do we destroy fortresses, speculations, and every lofty thing raised up against the knowledge of God? We identify every system of thought, philosophy, and even theology that attempts to eliminate or undermine God.

Soldiers of Christ, it is time to throw off timidity and any concern for what the world might think of us. It is time for all who call upon the name of Christ to be fearless. You will need to be courageous because when you stand against the "lofty ideas" and so-called knowledge that is the antithesis of true biblical knowledge and does in fact present itself as an enemy of God you will be attacked. These attacks will come from people you consider to be friends and even from your family.[55]

Let's start with a very touchy subject: the government indoctrination camps euphemistically called public schools.

How do we "square" God's commandments to have "no other Gods before Him" (Exodus 20:3) and "honor your father and mother" (Exodus 20:12) with a government education system that teaches children there is no God and that their parents are idiots if they prioritize their faith?

The average government school student will spend about 14,000 hours in a classroom before they graduate. This includes a great number of students who profess faith in Christ and are being reared in a Christian home. Statistics suggest that among these Christian students, each spends on average 1 hour a day interacting with their parents, and less than 3 hours per week at church services and associated activities.

Is it reasonable for us to assume that the Christian instruction they receive during time away from the government schools will outweigh the thousands of hours of anti-Christian perspectives they are bombarded with by the government school system as well as the media? What does God say about how He expects Christians to educate their children?

Are you prepared to tell your family, neighbors, co-workers, and friends that every belief system except Christian theism is a false belief system that will lead them to eternal separation from God their creator? If you are then that means you are prepared to tell them:

- That abortion is murder and is the modern day equivalent to a blood sacrifice to Satan.
- That transgenderism is only the latest sexual perversion that Satan has used to undermine Christianity.
- That our current path into debauchery and the ideology behind it will eventually include legalized pedophilia.
- That regardless of what laws Congress passes or the Supreme Court creates out of thin air homosexuals and lesbians will never be married in God's eyes?

---

[55] Matthew 10:21-22

- That live and let live is not a recipe for the long-term viability of any culture and that history has demonstrated that over and over again.
- That the righteousness of God when practiced by a people will exalt a nation but that sin allowed to flourish will destroy every people.[56]

I am amazed at the number of people who declare they are believers but will state unequivocally that they could be wrong about Jesus and that people like New Age heretic Oprah Winfrey could be right. I will say this as clearly as possible friends: God has spoken to us in His Son Jesus Christ[57] so that whoever will believe in Him will have eternal life.[58] There is no other name under heaven given among men by which we are saved.[59] God has supernaturally preserved a record of all of this so that we would know for certain that Jesus is THE Christ.[60] If you are not sure about Jesus then you don't know Him in saving faith.

The faithful soldier of Christ has put on Christ. Our identity is Christ. Galatians 3:26-27 says:

> "For you are all sons of God through faith in Jesus Christ. For all of you who were baptized into Christ have clothed yourselves with Christ."

A soldier of Christ endures hardship (Acts 9:16; 2 Timothy 2:3). A soldier of Christ recruits others (Matthew 28:18-20; the Gospels in their entirety). A soldier of Christ does not collaborate with the enemy (John 15:18).

I believe that the true Church of Jesus Christ, His body of born-again, blood bought, Holy Spirit empowered believers, MUST get their feet on the ground, get their hands "dirty" and get involved in the necessary activity of the Kingdom of God. We cannot sit back any longer.

---

[56] Proverbs 14:32-35
[57] Hebrews 11:1-4
[58] John 3:16
[59] Acts 4;12
[60] John 20:31

Chapter 9 - Pull Down the Strongholds: Prayer and Fasting

And He said to them, "This kind cannot come out by anything but prayer and fasting.
Mark 9:29 (KJV)

Jesus trained His disciples to proclaim the Gospel, to heal the diseased, and to subdue as well as cast out demons. The Gospel of Mark tells us that the disciples did this so successfully that King Herod thought Jesus was the resurrected John the Baptist.

This tells me a couple of things about the disciples and their first mission trip Jesus commissioned them to fulfill. First, there is power in the name of Jesus. Demons shuttered and shrank back at the mention of Jesus' name. Second, the disciples used the power and authority granted to them by Jesus and proclaimed everything they did in the name of Jesus. Jesus received all the credit and therefore all the glory and the honor.

We can know that the disciples were careful to do this because Mark 6:14 says that "King Herod heard of it, for His name had become well known, and people were saying, John the Baptist has risen from the dead, and that is why these miraculous powers are at work in Him."

Herod heard of all the disciples were doing – healing the sick, the diseased, and demon possessed and knew that it was happening by the power of the man named Jesus, whom he believed was the Baptist resurrected. Herod's fears were fueled because he knew John was a holy and righteous man (Mark 6:20). Yet pride won the day (Mark 6:26) and he acquiesced to having John murdered.

The story of John the Baptists' life is an extraordinary one. He was a man full of faith and unflinching courage. The disciples on the other hand seemed to be men of faith in some instances and men suffering from an inability to comprehend the most basic spiritual truths in others.

The Apostle Matthew records an event after the initial mission trip in which the disciples were not able to cast out a demon from a young man. Matthew 17:14-20 says:

> When they came to the crowd, a man came up to Jesus, falling on his knees before Him and saying, "Lord, have mercy on my son, for he is a lunatic and is very ill; for he often falls into the fire and often into the water. I brought him to Your disciples, and they could not cure him." And Jesus answered and said, "You unbelieving and perverted generation, how long shall I be with you? How long shall I put up with you? Bring him here to Me." And Jesus rebuked him, and the demon came out of him, and the boy was cured at once. Then the disciples came to Jesus privately and said, "Why could we not drive it out?" And He said to them, "Because of the littleness of your faith; for truly I say to you, if you have faith the size of a mustard seed, you will say to this mountain, 'Move from here to there,' and it will move; and nothing will be impossible to you.

Jesus chastises the disciples for "littleness of faith." But then turns around and says all that is necessary is faith the size of a mustard seed. This appears to be inconsistent in the least until you understand what it is Jesus is telling them in context.

Jesus was always teaching the disciples. Every situation presented a teaching moment that Jesus utilized to strengthen the disciples faith. This was all done with His impending crucifixion, resurrection, and ascension in view. The day was rapidly approaching when the disciples would have to have the faith to do all that Jesus taught them without Him being by their side.

In this particular case Jesus was accompanied by Peter, John, and James to the top of a mountain. We read in Matthew 17:2 that Jesus was transfigured or transformed before them such that His face shined like the sun and His garments became white as light. What were the other nine disciples doing? They were below attempting to cast a demon out of a young man brought to them by his father. When Jesus and the three disciples came down the mountain they are met by a desperate father who told Jesus the nine disciples were unable to do anything to help his son (Matthew 17:16).

This led Jesus to some very frank words in Matthew 17:17, 21. Now what does this mean? Jesus is telling the disciples to persevere in prayer. He is telling them that they can't give up just because something doesn't happen the moment they pray, a lesson that would greatly benefit us all. Keep praying, stick with it and as you do your faith will grow. That's the lesson of the mustard seed: not that it is small, as Jesus had already commented on the littleness of their faith, but rather the mustard seed is meant to illustrate for them the vastness of the potential and possibility of God answering their prayers if they will be persistent.

Then, to drive this point home, Jesus said if they had a growing faith, similar to a mustard seed, they would overcome the most difficult situations they would face. He used the metaphor of a mountain, something the disciples were familiar with as it was a well-known Jewish idiom of the day. If they persevered in their faith and did not give up then the mountains of trouble that would surely come in their lifetimes would be overcome. His statement "and nothing will be impossible to you" was spoken within the context of representing Christ to the world.

Persistent prayer is a hallmark of the believer. James says that the effective prayer of a righteous man can accomplish much.[61] I believe that many of you reading this book have labored in prayer for many years on behalf of loved ones, co-workers, and neighbors who need to trust in Jesus for the forgiveness of sin and to be born again. No doubt someone prayed for you to be saved as well.

---

[61] James 5:16

Men Let's Get Specific

Guys, let's talk about persistent prayer. This isn't a beat-down or a shame-fest meant to cajole you into spending more time in prayer. The congregation I have the blessing to pastor knows that this is not a tactic I employ. Shaming people into doing something never works in the long run.

Instead men, I want you to consider why you should pray for your wives AND more importantly, what your frame of reference should be. Praying for our wives should be a top priority in our lives and taking the correct approach based on a correct understanding of why we must pray for our wives will yield much fruit.

What is that right approach? Men, we are to pray for our wives so that WE can be changed. I can almost hear all the "what?" questions right now. "What do you mean pray for my wife so that I can change? She is the one that needs to be changed!"

Here is a spiritual principle to try on guys: you only have control over your responses. You cannot control the responses of other people. In fact, you will never see the changes you want in your wife until you become the change you want to see. The old adage that warns not to point fingers at others for their faults because there are at least three fingers pointing back at you comes to mind here.

So, how does praying for your wife with the proper attitude change you? Because praying for your wife with the right attitude will soften your heart. I know this is true from personal experience. You cannot honestly pray for someone you are mad at or aggravated with. I have counseled many men over the years to put this principle to the test. My counsel to them has been this: the next time you and your wife find yourselves in a discussion that is heading "out of bounds," have the courage to stop, look your wife in the eyes, take her hands, and say "let's pray."

When you pour your heart out for your wife, and when you seek God and ask Him to encourage her to be all that she can be in Him, I guarantee you God will show you ways that you are hindering her in that quest. Men, we are sinners and more often than we want to admit we display a callousness toward our wives that directly undermines the very character qualities we desire to see in her.

Men when we pray for our wives to be all that God wants them to be our heart attitudes toward them will change. Has there been strife and discord in the relationship? It is impossible to hold onto a hurt while praying earnestly for God to move and work in our wives. And when we do ask God to move in our wives lives He will begin by showing us what part we must play in that process.

This will also draw our attention to her needs, desires, strengths, and weaknesses. We will begin to see where we can step in and offer help or volunteer to take something off her plate. Guys, I don't need to remind you that we can get caught up in our busy lives of work, schedules, and deadlines. Not to mention the children's activities and church related events. It is easy to forget that our wives have struggles too and would see your unsolicited offer to help as a huge encouragement.

In this process of praying for our wives we will experience change in our own attitude and will begin to sense our hearts being more closely aligned with our wives hearts. Men, it is a commonly accepted truth that women seek a deeper emotional bond with their husbands, deeper than many men realize. You've been put on notice now so what are you going to do in response?

Being a godly husband is a daunting task when rightly understood. Our role is to provide strong, consistent, righteous leadership that demonstrates patience under fire, kindness as a first priority, and perhaps most importantly self-control. Being a husband does not give you the title of dictator nor the authority to "lord" anything over your wife. If those are your behaviors, then you are sowing to the wind and as the Bible says you will reap a whirlwind of trouble.

What About Fasting?

I believe that one of the most important things we can do is fast on a regular basis. When we pray and join that prayer with fasting it creates a very formidable weapon against the evil one.

Fasting is a humbling endeavor but it is also a tremendously rewarding spiritual discipline. Here is what Jesus said about fasting:

> "Whenever you fast, do not put on a gloomy face as the hypocrites *do*, for they neglect their appearance so that they will be noticed by men when they are fasting. Truly I say to you, they have their reward in full. But you, when you fast, anoint your head and wash your face so that your fasting will not be noticed by men, but by your Father who is in secret; and your Father who sees *what is done* in secret will reward you." (Matthew 6:16-18)

The context for this teaching is found in verse 1 of the same chapter. Jesus said, "Beware of practicing your righteousness before men to be noticed by them; otherwise you have no reward with your Father who is in heaven."

Here we read that fasting is seen by God and when it is done from the heart our Father in heaven rewards us. I can't think of anything more exciting than receiving God's favor, His goodness, and His riches when I simply deny myself a physical desire for a period of time while asking Him to draw me closer to Him. However, I believe the reward being spoken of in this passage is not merely the generic favor of God. I believe it is God's specific answers to your prayers that occasioned the fast in the first place.

I also want you to understand the biblical picture of fasting because today in America fasting has become the newest health craze. There are now dozens of fasts each with their own name and alleged Bible verse to justify it. What is missing from all of these is a key attitude and disposition. See if you pick up on it from these Scriptures:

> When I heard these words, I sat down and wept and mourned for days; and I was fasting and praying before the God of heaven. (Nehemiah 1:4)

Now on the twenty-fourth day of this month the sons of Israel assembled with fasting, in sackcloth and with dirt upon them. (Nehemiah 9:1)

In each and every province where the command and decree of the king came, there was great mourning among the Jews, with fasting, weeping and wailing; and many lay in sackcloth and ashes. (Esther 4:3)

to establish these days of Purim at their appointed times, just as Mordecai the Jew and Queen Esther had established for them, and just as they had established for themselves and for their descendants with instructions for their times of fasting and their lamentations. (Esther 9:31)

But as for me, when they were sick, my clothing was sackcloth; I humbled my soul with fasting, and my prayer kept returning to my bosom. (Psalm 35:13)

So I gave my attention to the Lord God to seek *Him by* prayer and supplications, with fasting, sackcloth and ashes. (Daniel 9:3)

"Yet even now," declares the Lord, "Return to Me with all your heart, And with fasting, weeping and mourning. (Joel 2:12)

While they were ministering to the Lord and fasting, the Holy Spirit said, "Set apart for Me Barnabas and Saul for the work to which I have called them." (Acts 13:2)

When they had appointed elders for them in every church, having prayed with fasting, they commended them to the Lord in whom they had believed. (Acts 14:23)

What do you see as the prevailing attitude of those that fasted and prayed? If you said they were concerned to varying degrees about the circumstances surrounding them and they knew that only God resolves situations for their good and His glory then you are correct. Fasting is one aspect of serious spiritual warfare. Engaging in a fast coupled with prayer is your heart cry to God for Him to move on your behalf or on behalf of others.

And this is a key spiritual principle. If you are not pursuing God before you start a fast chances are you won't be when you end it either. Fasting does not create your desired reality like some kind of magical elixir. God desires obedience much more than sacrifice. A broken and contrite heart is the best offering we can bring to Him (Psalm 51:16-17). Giving God a stiff arm in your life renders your fasting ineffective.

Therefore entering into a time of fasting is meant to remove obstacles and distractions so that you can hear from God. Fasting is an act of worship accompanied by humility as you submit yourself before God and ask Him to guide you in more understanding, more wisdom, and more opportunities to represent him in the world in which you live. Fasting is a time of cleansing from the sin that both entangles you and keeps you from obeying God faithfully.

A well-known passage in Isaiah dealing with fasting highlights the type of fast God is interested in. Isaiah 58:3-4 says:

> Why have we fasted and You do not see?
> *Why* have we humbled ourselves and You do not notice?
> Behold, on the day of your fast you find *your* desire,
> And drive hard all your workers.
> "Behold, you fast for contention and strife and to strike with a wicked fist.
> You do not fast like *you do* today to make your voice heard on high.

The Jewish people were complaining to God that He didn't answer their petitions and prayers during the times of their fasting. He told them plainly that they were not seeking Him in their fast but rather their own desires. They lived disobedient and rebellious lives. In other words they gave God a stiff arm but expected their fasts to move Him to action.

God criticizes their attempt at appearing to mourn their sin and seek His face in 58:5:

> Is it a fast like this which I choose, a day for a man to humble himself?
> Is it for bowing one's head like a reed
> And for spreading out sackcloth and ashes as a bed?
> Will you call this a fast, even an acceptable day to the LORD?

In His graciousness God reminds them what He seeks:

> Is this not the fast which I choose,
> To loosen the bonds of wickedness,
> To undo the bands of the yoke,
> And to let the oppressed go free
> And break every yoke?
> Is it not to divide your bread with the hungry
> And bring the homeless poor into the house;
> When you see the naked, to cover him;
> And not to hide yourself from your own flesh?
> Then your light will break out like the dawn,
> And your recovery will speedily spring forth;
> And your righteousness will go before you;
> The glory of the LORD will be your rear guard.[62]

What does all of this have to do with the Church and shepherds in general? We live in a culture that is on the go constantly. Our schedules are filled to the brim and are often overbooked. This results in stress, anxiety, and desperation. Christians just like their unsaved friends and neighbors increasingly look for quick fixes and easy answers to their concerns. This causes us to view spiritual matters in much the same fashion. But the spiritual realm does not operate by our clock. Spiritual disciplines such as prayer, supplication, and fasting, take time. God will answer the prayers of His children but He does so in His timing.

Churches must get back to spending time in corporate prayer. Shepherds must encourage believers to spend time in prayer individually, with their spouse, with their children, and with others wherever and whenever the opportunity presents itself. The problems that America faces today must be addressed in prayer first and foremost. Only after much prayer and fasting will the people of God be ready to put feet to the ground and attack the enemy strongholds head on. Rushing into battle without prayer is a short-sighted and ill-advised strategy for God's people.

---

[62] Isaiah 58:6-8

Chapter 10 – Strengthen the Body: Fortifying the Home Base

Now, therefore, fear the LORD and serve Him in sincerity and truth; and put away the gods which your fathers served beyond the River and in Egypt, and serve the LORD. If it is disagreeable in your sight to serve the LORD, choose for yourselves today whom you will serve: whether the gods which your fathers served which were beyond the River, or the gods of the Amorites in whose land you are living; but as for me and my house, we will serve the LORD.[63]

Let me begin this chapter with a bold and encouraging statement: apostasy is rising rapidly and the remnant body of believers is growing stronger. A clash is coming. This is certainly bold but is it encouraging? I believe it is and because both of those things are true, I wonder if we are about to experience a Joshua moment?

I believe a clear division already exists between the visible, organized Church and the remnant body of believers. The most telling part of Joshua 24:14-15 is not "but as for me and my house we will serve the Lord." It is instead, "If it is disagreeable in your sight to serve the Lord, choose for yourselves today whom you will serve…"

---

[63]Joshua 24:14-15

Why would Joshua say "If it is disagreeable in your sight to serve the Lord" in v.15? He was speaking to Israel. Wasn't Israel God's people? Please note in v.14 Joshua tells Israel to: fear the LORD; serve Him and Him alone; and to do so sincerely, as well as truthfully. This rebuke was necessary because much of Israel was not doing any of this. They were fake believers who worshipped demons in the form of the idols of Egypt.

A shaking, a sifting, and a revealing have come to the American Church brothers and sisters. We need a refresher on the goal, purpose, and mission of the faithful. Spoiler alert: it's not your happiness and personal sense of well-being. Consider this your strategy briefing, a "Triple E" learning session of Exhortation, Encouragement, and Equipping.

The visible Church can no longer be understood as the literal, spiritual, and actual body of Christ. There are hundreds and thousands of false converts – tares – sitting in pews all across America every Sunday. Politicians, and even some Christians proclaim we must take America back! I say in response that you better take back the Church first or America won't be worth taking back. Within the Church we sing "Rescue the Perishing" but has it never dawned on those singing this song that the perishing are sitting or standing right beside them every time they gather together as the visible body of Christ?

Our focal passage is found in 1 Corinthians 1:13 where the Apostle Paul is taking the Corinthians to task for being carnal and divisive. His question to them raises several questions for us. First can the body of Christ be divided and still function? Second what is the implication of this for the Gospel witness of the Church? Finally how will God still accomplish His purposes through the visible Church when they are in such disarray?

The Visible is Often Not the Real

Jesus told an interesting parable that illustrates the condition of the Church today.

Jesus presented another parable to them, saying, "The kingdom of heaven may be compared to a man who sowed good seed in his field. But while his men were sleeping, his enemy came and sowed tares among the wheat, and went away. But when the wheat sprouted and bore grain, then the tares became evident also. The slaves of the landowner came and said to him, 'Sir, did you not sow good seed in your field? How then does it have tares?' And he said to them, 'An enemy has done this!' The slaves said to him, 'Do you want us, then, to go and gather them up?' But he said, 'No; for while you are gathering up the tares, you may uproot the wheat with them. Allow both to grow together until the harvest; and in the time of the harvest I will say to the reapers, "First gather up the tares and bind them in bundles to burn them up; but gather the wheat into my barn."[64]

True Christians struggle to explain how the Church has become so compromised today. Just this week I heard news about the National Cathedral in Washington DC, which bills itself as "a catalyst for spiritual harmony in our nation, reconciliation among faiths, and compassion in the world."[65] Apparently those that manage this structure and its many operations thought the best way to achieve spiritual harmony through melding all faiths into one for a more compassionate expression of faith was to strike every masculine expression for God in the Bible. This is the same organization that has already declared homosexual and lesbian "unions" right and proper and has followed that up with ordaining homosexuals and lesbians to their view of Gospel ministry.

The sad stories do not stop there. This Episcopalian congregation embraces the wholesale slaughter of the unborn through abortion on demand including partial birth abortion, they support social justice groups that are little more than terrorist fronts, the divestiture from any Israeli company, and every other leftist propaganda that is part of the long and growing list of virtue signaling Luciferianism.

---

[64] Matthew 13:24-30
[65] See https://cathedral.org/about-the-cathedral/mission-and-vision Accessed March 14, 2018.

I'm not singling out the Episcopalians. This widespread apostasy has compromised many denominations as well as many groups that identify as non-denominational. I could just as easily be speaking about the Methodists, the Lutherans, or the Southern Baptists who once were known as the fighting Baptists but now are called by many in their ranks the compromising Baptists.

There is indeed a dividing happening in the Church of Jesus Christ today. I see the chaff being thrown to the wind so that the wheat might be identified. The Holy Spirit is showing us who the real believers are. We call ourselves the remnant because in contrast to the visible Church we are a small remnant, a tiny percentage of the whole. Once again the visible Church is not representative of true biblical Christianity. Much of the visible Church is a weak, fractured, and anemic facade that long ago left the narrow path of truth.

Can the Body of Christ be Divided and Still Function Properly?

Paul wrote to the Corinthian churches in order to correct them on many things. One of their aberrant attitudes was their divisive rivalries and factions. He pointed out to them that all eyes should be on Jesus. He told them that Christ cannot be divided.[66] That the Corinthians were trying to do so made it necessary for Paul to ask the question. The body cannot function if Christ is divided. What he meant by this was that Christ is not the champion of your cause if your goals are in conflict with what He has already revealed to us through His Spirit and His Word. Trying to co-op Christ to shore up your perspective is an unnecessary and dangerous thing to do.

Regrettable, this very thing has been happening all across America for several decades now. The Church has been splintered by those who have left Christ behind to chase all sorts of culturally acceptable dogma. Ironically some of

[66] 1 Corinthians 1:13

them still attempt to march under Christ's banner. The still wear the vestments albeit with rainbow sashes and cords. They still stand behind pulpits week after week but what comes out of their mouths are blatant lies, deliberate misrepresentations, and fantasies of their own imagination. We cannot strengthen the local body of Christ followers until we remove the Baal worshippers from our midst. Really Pastor Mike? Yes, really folks. Why do we tolerate the demonically controlled people in our midst? Have we become so tone deaf to God and the Holy Spirit in us that we just shrug our shoulders and succumb to the lie of powerlessness?

Let me make a comparison for you. I'm teaching through the Gospel of Mark right now and last week arrived at Chapter 7:24. It is an interesting section for a number of reasons but for my purposes I want to call your attention to the fact that Jesus went into a Gentile area and there was approached by a Syrophoenician woman. Matthew says she was a Canaanite woman which was also true.[67] If you know your Old Testament history then you will recall that the Israelites were commanded to cleanse the land of the Canaanites when they began their conquest under Joshua.

The reason for this was because the Canaanites had become a wicked people who had soaked the land with blood for generations. The Canaanites worshipped Baal and consequently engaged in rampant incest since Baal was said to have had sex with his mother, sister, and daughter. Adultery was routine because Baal worship was a fertility cult complete with temple prostitutes. The result of these sexual perversions and spontaneous orgies was children and thus child sacrifice was included as a means to dispose of the inconvenience of children under the cover of satisfying the Canaanite god of the underworld Moloch.[68] Homosexuality and bestiality were an accepted and normal practice enshrined in Canaanite literature, poetry, and law.[69]

---

[67] Matthew 15:22

[68] My friend Doug Overmyer wrote a great piece on the connection between abortion and the Old Testament pagan child sacrificing rituals of the Canaanites to Moloch. *Parenting in the Land of Molech* can be found here - http://www.drmikespaulding.com/?p=1843

[69] See for example Stephanie Dalley, "Erra and Ishum IV," *Myths from Mesopotamia* (Oxford: Oxford University, 1989), 305. Harry A. Hofner, Jr., "Incest, Sodomy and Bestiaity in the Ancient Near East," in *Orient and Occident: Essays Presented to Cyrus H. Gordon on the Occasion of His Sixty-fifth Birthday,* ed. Harry A. Hoffner, Jr. (Neukirchen Vluyn Germany: Neukirchen

Of course, their wickedness all flowed out of their idolatry. Their refusal to bow their knee to Yahweh and repent of their abominations drove them in the opposite direction – they loved what Yahweh hated and hated what Yahweh loved. Israel's sad history of idolatry and spiritual adultery against Yahweh was a result of their refusal to blot out the plague of the Canaanites from the land God gave them.

I have shared the despicable behavior and wanton disregard for God and His perfect law by the Canaanites for a specific reason: the very same things are being promoted today by those professing to love God! Planned Parenthood is a child sacrificing beast and the soil of America cries out with the blood of sixty million murdered innocent unborn children while so-called believers parade about with their signs pledging allegiance to this modern day Moloch. Advocates of all manner of sexual perversion have conquered most of the so-called mainline denominations and have turned them into little more than organisms for the promotion of things God hates.

However, the true body of Christ cannot be divided because it will remain faithful to Christ and to His Word. It will not tolerate the agendas of the ungodly and will oppose them at every turn. It may well be that the remnant will need to leave compromised churches. Some may choose to fight and cast out the evil doers from their midst. Regardless of which strategy remnant believers use Christ will be glorified and lifted up among His true people.

What of the Gospel ministry? How will the true Church respond in this time of spiritual upheaval within the visible Church? One thing we must remain clear on is the Gospel message. Jesus saves all who truly repent and turn to Him in faith for the forgiveness of their sin. This certainly includes wayward believers, but we must not compromise the Gospel. We must give no cover or quarter to those who willingly reject the Gospel for another Gospel of their vain imaginations.[70] That means we must be extremely clear

---

Verlag, 1973), 82, 187-188. Mark S. Smith, trans. *Ugaritic Narrative Poetry*, ed. Simon B. Parker (Atlanta: Society of Biblical Literature, 1997), 148.
[70] 2 Corinthians 11:4

and boldly transparent about the wanton apostasy that has seized the visible Church.

Make no apology for the truth friends. The truth of Jesus Christ sets the captives of Satan's deceptions free.

America is in disarray like never before. The forces of evil are flexing their muscles and enjoying this season of perceived success but make no mistake friends: God is not mocked.[71] The harvest that the apostates will reap is death and eternal separation.

I believe that God will accomplish His purposes today in spite of the apostasy of the visible Church. I believe that God is strengthening His people to stand in the gap for Him. The most sure-fire way the remnant will persevere is to stay focused on the true Gospel of Jesus Christ.

Get the Gospel Right

"and others were tortured, not accepting their release, so that they might obtain a better resurrection; and others experienced mockings and scourgings, yes, also chains and imprisonment. They were stoned, they were sawn in two, they were tempted, they were put to death with the sword; they went about in sheepskins, in goatskins, being destitute, afflicted, ill-treated (men of whom the world was not worthy), wandering in deserts and mountains and caves and holes in the ground." [72]

This passage from Hebrews is speaking about the saints of old and the tribulation they endured. The Bible does not tell us their fates but other literary sources do tell us the fates of many of the Apostles: Matthew was beheaded, James was beaten to death, Paul was beheaded, Peter was crucified as was Andrew. Thomas was run through with a spear and Luke was hanged. Talk about a message that is out of step with the modern revisionist gospel hucksters who love to paint a rosy picture of gospel prosperity for every believer who has enough of the right kind of faith.

---

[71] Galatians 6:7-8
[72] Hebrews 11:35-38

The reason I bring these things to your attention today is because it has become wildly popular for Christians to speak of God's great design and purpose for everyone. And what most purveyors of this message mean by these messages is that God wants to give you stuff. Evangelism for many amounts to little more than telling potential converts that "God will solve all your problems. Why not give Him a try?"

If you're like me you probably know someone who is battling cancer right now. Perhaps a dear friend is suffering through the pain of a disintegrating marriage or battling depression due to the loss of a job. If coming to God is supposed to solve a person's problems as many Christians claim today, then why are those that are already trusting in God experiencing such difficult circumstances?

In our own time we are seeing the persecution of Christians around the world. The Islamic State and radical Islam continue to enslave, rape, and murder Christians in Africa, Iraq, Syria, France, England, India, and elsewhere. How does the modern evangelistic "hook" of God's wonderful plan play out there? Is the persecution and martyrdom of Middle East believers "their best life now?"

Friends, the Christian life is not a bed of roses and pretending it is doesn't match up with what the Bible has to say. Jesus told those who followed Him that "Brother will betray brother to death, and a father his child; and children will rise up against parents and cause them to be put to death. You will be hated by all because of My name, but it is the one who has endured to the end who will be saved" (Matthew 10:21-22).

Friends, being a Christian means suffering for the sake of Jesus' name. Telling people that God has a wonderful plan for their lives and will solve all their problems actually results in false converts because the Gospel is good news only to those who have recognized that they are separated from a holy God by their sin. Making professions of faith on the basis of wanting God to give you your best life now, will result in facing God's judgment later. This will be a horrifying truth for all those who have trusted in a false Gospel, and should be cause for remorse and repentance for all those offering such a false Gospel.

Remember the words of Jesus as recorded in Matthew 7:21-23: "Not everyone who says to Me, 'Lord, Lord,' will enter the kingdom of heaven . . . . Many will say to Me on that day, 'Lord, Lord, did we not prophesy in Your name, and in Your name cast out demons, and in Your name perform many miracles?" And then I will declare to them, 'I never knew you; Depart from Me, you who practice lawlessness." There are many people who are going to hear these terrifying words because they have accepted a false gospel of demonic origin. Friends, let's get the Gospel right, because it is the true Gospel that saves and transforms lives.

Chapter 11 – Know the Scriptures: Feeding the Inner Man

Listen to the word of the LORD, O sons of Israel,
For the LORD has a case against the inhabitants of the land,
Because there is no faithfulness or kindness
Or knowledge of God in the land. Hosea 4:1

How many of you have heard the cliché "doctrine divides" put forth as an excuse for not teaching the Bible? If you said no you are among a small minority. An overwhelming majority of churches will not take a firm stand on much of anything today, and that is especially true of biblical teaching that says the culturally elevated anti-God doctrines of demons are exactly that – products of hell.

It defies reason and logic that churches abandon the truth of the Scriptures and choose instead to be swept along by the cultural winds that are becoming whirlwinds of destruction. Christian Watchmen have been sounding an alarm for some time now but most Christians are not listening.

Abandoning Doctrine Has Severe Consequences

At some point I'm sure that all pastor's and ministry leaders understood that the Gospel is doctrine. The New Testament writers stressed this point and encouraged believers to remember to stick with what they received. Consider these exhortations:

> holding fast the faithful word which is in accordance with the teaching, so that he will be able both to exhort in sound doctrine and to refute those who contradict. (Titus 1:9)[73]

> If anyone advocates a different doctrine and does not agree with sound words, those of our Lord Jesus Christ, and with the doctrine conforming to godliness, he is conceited *and* understands nothing. (1 Timothy 6:3-4a)

> Pay close attention to yourself and to your teaching; persevere in these things, for as you do this you will ensure salvation both for yourself and for those who hear you. (1 Timothy 4:16)

Here is a very simple yet apparently lost truth: in order to persevere in the faith we must be reminded constantly of the sound doctrine that underpins the faith itself. In fact we can take this a step farther. In order to believe and to be genuinely born again you must believe in the Lord Jesus Christ as He is shown to us in the Bible. Again sound doctrine is imperative here because sound doctrine is the Gospel. Forgetting this has resulted in all sorts of nonsense in the Church today.

The teaching of sound doctrine supports the firm foundation of Jesus Christ. That forms the basis for a good definition and foundation for the Church: a group of people who have professed, confessed, repented of their sin, sought and received forgiveness of their sin, have placed their faith in Jesus Christ for the salvation of their souls, committed to living their lives as disciples of Jesus Christ by the power of the Holy Spirit, and focused on gathering together with other believers who have done the same things for the purposes of worshipping their Creator, honoring their Messiah and Savior, and learning from the sound doctrine of the Word of God.

---

[73] This is part of a larger exhortation to those who serve as Elders. Note that church leaders are to (1) know what constitutes sound doctrine and (2) refute those who stray from it.

We see this very thing in many places in the Scriptures. Peter after preaching the message of Yeshua Ha Maschiach as the Messiah and Savior of Israel and the world, told the people listening to repent and turn to Jesus the Christ in faith.

> Now when they heard *this*, they were pierced to the heart, and said to Peter and the rest of the apostles, "Brethren, what shall we do?" Peter *said* to them, "Repent, and each of you be baptized in the name of Jesus Christ for the forgiveness of your sins; and you will receive the gift of the Holy Spirit. For the promise is for you and your children and for all who are far off, as many as the Lord our God will call to Himself." And with many other words he solemnly testified and kept on exhorting them, saying, "Be saved from this perverse generation!" So then, those who had received his word were baptized; and that day there were added about three thousand souls. They were **continually devoting themselves to the apostles' teaching** and to fellowship, to the breaking of bread and to prayer. (Acts 2:37-42; emphasis added)

What constituted the Apostle's teaching? All that Jesus taught them and that they faithful wrote down under the inspiration of the Holy Spirit.

> but you will receive power when the Holy Spirit has come upon you; and you shall be **My witnesses** both in Jerusalem, and in all Judea and Samaria, and even to the remotest part of the earth. (Acts 1:8; emphasis added)[74]

> But the eleven disciples proceeded to Galilee, to the mountain which Jesus had designated. When they saw Him, they worshiped *Him*; but some were doubtful. And Jesus came up and spoke to them, saying, "All authority has been given to Me in heaven and on earth. Go therefore and make disciples of all the nations, baptizing them in the name of the Father and the Son and the Holy Spirit, **teaching them to observe all that I commanded you**; and lo, I am with you always, even to the end of the age." (Matthew 28:16-20; emphasis added)

---

[74] The meaning is that the disciples would tell others what Jesus taught them.

For I delivered to you as of first importance **what I also received**, that Christ died for our sins according to the Scriptures, and that He was buried, and that He was raised on the third day according to the Scriptures, and that He appeared to Cephas, then to the twelve. After that He appeared to more than five hundred brethren at one time, most of whom remain until now, but some have fallen asleep; then He appeared to James, then to all the apostles; and last of all, as to one untimely born, **He appeared to me also.** (1 Corinthians 15:3-8; emphasis added)

But even if we, or an angel from heaven, should preach to you a gospel contrary **to what we have preached to you,** he is to be accursed! As we have said before, so I say again now, if any man is preaching to you a gospel contrary **to what you received,** he is to be accursed! (Galatians 1:8-9; emphasis added)

So remember what you have received and heard; and keep it, and repent. Therefore if you do not wake up, I will come like a thief, and you will not know at what hour I will come to you. (Revelation 3:3; emphasis added)

Of particular importance here is to remember that the writers of the New Testament were writing within the life times of eye witnesses to all they wrote. Refuting any detail would have been trivial, but it never happened for one simple reason: what the Gospel writers recorded was the widely acknowledged truth.

Dr. Ken Johnson has written a fantastic book that chronicles what the disciples of the Apostles taught.[75] In his thorough study, Johnson presents us with many compelling arguments concluding that the teaching of the early church fathers was very much in line with what Jesus taught the Apostles who subsequently taught the later disciples such as Ignatius, Irenaeus, and Polycarp.

---

[75] Ken Johnson, *Ancient Church Fathers: What the Disciples of the Apostles Taught* (Self Published, 2010).

I state all of this to make unambiguously clear that neglecting doctrine will and has resulted in the spiritual death of churches and believers. There is a reason many churches are closing: many have left the sure foundation of Jesus Christ and the teaching of His Word. Christians will not grow in holiness or in any of the fruits of the Spirit if he or she is not nurtured consistently in the teaching of the Bible. There is no short cut to spiritual maturity.

Can we agree that there is little to no knowledge of the Lord in America today? Don't you find that ironic and more than a little troubling? I certainly do, not least because there are churches in nearly every city in America. Granted some of them are not Christian churches and they use that deception to lure people to them. However, we also have an abundance of Christian ministries, radio stations, television stations, campus ministries, ministries focused exclusively on athletes in different sports, and the list goes on.

But the general population of America is becoming more disconnected from our Christian heritage than ever before. I believe this is happening simply because the Church has withdrawn from its primary missions of outreach, evangelism, and witnessing. At the same time the Church has abdicated its responsibility there has been a great influx of other religious belief systems and the rise of multifarious groups within America. For example, Islam, Hinduism, and Buddhism are all growing in adherents in America. So are pagans, Wiccans, and New Agers although this is no longer a properly descriptive classification since so many different groups can be categorized as New Age.

One prominent reason Christians do not bother to witness is because the thought of having to answer why they believe what they believe scares them to death. They say they care about lost people but they won't take the time to study the Bible in order to understand why they believe what they believe. Thus they are not capable of giving a reasonable and satisfying answer to questions raised by the lost.

My prayer is that Christians will understand the ground they have given up in their retreat from the secular battlefield and begin to prepare themselves for the battle that is already raging all around them. Once you know why you believe what you believe the next thing you must do is go tell everyone that they must turn from their sin and serve the Lord Jesus Christ before His soon return.

Knowing why you believe what you believe will better prepare you to give an explanation for the hope that is in you.[76] Rescue the perishing is not just a song for our services anymore. It is a call to action for the remnant Church both inside and outside the walls of our meeting places.

---

[76] 1 Peter 3:15

Chapter 12 – Stop Cannibalizing One Another: Love Defines the Body of Christ

For you were called to freedom, brethren; only do not turn your freedom into an opportunity for the flesh, but through love serve one another. ¹⁴ For the whole Law is fulfilled in one word, in the statement, "YOU SHALL LOVE YOUR NEIGHBOR AS YOURSELF." ¹⁵ But if you bite and devour one another, take care that you are not consumed by one another. Galatians 5:13-15

God has impressed upon me a word for a battered and bruised reed: encourage the weary. Encourage the remnant body of Jesus Christ. They are battered and bruised yet remain standing. Encourage the remnant body of Jesus Christ who wear the scars of battle with honor and have determined in their hearts before God as their witness that they will run neither from evil or the many pawns the enemy has captured and is even now using to advance his agenda across America.

My wife Kathy and I were reading our morning devotional together recently and we came upon one that said something like "people don't need to be reminded again and again of their present plight as much as they need to be reminded of the glorious God we serve. People need a fresh vision of who God is and His present helps to them, much more than they need a reminder of the darkness of the present age."

Amen! On my drive to work that morning I passed a church with an LED sign - one of those really bright signs you can't help but look at especially in the dark - that said "Encourage the weary. Isaiah 50:4-5" You better believe as soon as I got to work I picked up my Bible and turned to that passage. Here is what it says:

> The Lord GOD has given Me the tongue of disciples,
> That I may know how to sustain the weary one with a word.
> He awakens *Me* morning by morning,
> He awakens My ear to listen as a disciple.
> The Lord GOD has opened My ear;
> And I was not disobedient
> Nor did I turn back.

I considered this in light of the current state of affairs within the church and I was reminded of Galatians 5:13. I think it is now more than ever appropriate to remind readers of this passage because of where we are today as God's people.

> For you were called to freedom, brethren; only *do* not *turn* your freedom into an opportunity for the flesh Galatians.

The word opportunity in that verse is from the Greek *aphorme*. It is used in a military sense and it speaks of a base of operation. In other words Paul is saying don't make your flesh the base of your operation. Don't say I'm a Christian, and I'm going to go to heaven, so I can behave as badly as I want. Instead, he says you are not made free to use your liberty as a springboard for the flesh.

Not everyone who bears the name Christian is one. Look at their fruit. Christian freedom does no injury to a brother or sister. – Galatians 5:13 says to use your liberty to love one another by serving them. WOW. "Serve" there is the word for "bond slavery."

Let's finish this passage with Galatians 5:14-17. Too many Christians who are no doubt saved, and are going to be in the presence of God one day because of their faith in Christ, are nonetheless behaving in this world like loving their brethren doesn't matter as long as they are correct on their points of view. They are intent on devouring one another and causing untold harm to the body of Christ in the process, but as long as they believe they are right nothing else matters.

Instead of devouring one another Paul says in Galatians 5:25 that we are to walk by the Spirit. What does that mean? It means that we "put on the Lord Jesus Christ."

- It means living a Christ-like life.
- It means being obedient and submissive to the point that we have the "mind of Christ."
- It means the Holy Spirit dominates our thought life.
- It means to walk by the Holy Spirit and to live a life visibly saturated with Jesus.

The flesh fights against these critical behaviors and attitudes at every turn so how do we reconcile this conflict with the exhortations in the Scriptures to contend for the faith? Jude 1-7. Stop blasting your fellow believers. STOP IT!

No one has designated you the depository of all truth. Stop devouring people because they hold to a different understanding of eschatological things. I could care less what your view of the rapture is or whether you believe in a literal or figurative thousand year reign of Christ. Those things are irrelevant to the greater task at hand: we must occupy until Jesus returns, whenever that will be. That is the call upon all Christians in every age. OCCUPY! Get up out of the pew, put on the armor of God and get out into the streets!

The Church will be great again when it makes God their complete focus again. Without making the pulpit great again by making sure that pastors are men of unbridled passion for Jesus Christ who will bend the knee to no earthly thing and will give all including their dying breath for the glory of our great God and Father, the Church will never be great again and America will continue into the abyss unaided by the very thing God has designated salt and light: the body of Jesus Christ.

Be That Man or Woman!

I was speaking with my friend Chance Gibson, owner of American Survival Wholesale recently. I shared with him the idea for this book and a little bit of background on the call I was sensing to write it. He said, "Pastor Mike, I have a few words for you that the Lord spoke to me." Chance proceeded to say these words: honor, courage, humility, dedication, loyalty, empathy, determination, righteousness, taking authority, leadership, and training. After reciting these words Chance said he believes they mean that Christians are to have a warrior mindset.

How do these things apply? What are we to have a warrior mindset about? Let's start with the Apostle Paul's exhortation to the Corinthian believers:

> For consider your calling, brethren, that there were not many wise according to the flesh, not many mighty, not many noble; but God has chosen the foolish things of the world to shame the wise, and God has chosen the weak things of the world to shame the things which are strong, and the base things of the world and the despised God has chosen, the things that are not, so that He may nullify the things that are, so that no man may boast before God. But by His doing you are in Christ Jesus, who became to us wisdom from God, and righteousness and sanctification, and redemption, so that, just as it is written, "LET HIM WHO BOASTS, BOAST IN THE LORD."[77]

I see Paul speaking prophetically about the remnant Church of today. Paul speaks of that which is not at that time but that would be raised in God's timing to both nullify the things that are in verse 28 and to shame the things that are strong in verse 27. I believe that prophetically Paul is speaking to our times and to the believers who remain faithful to the Lord Jesus Christ. The remnant body of believers – those who are not wise according to the flesh, not mighty, not noble by the world's standards – have been chosen by God has chosen us to shame the wise and strong.

The point I'm making here friends is that God has chosen us to be His vessels of honor in this time in America's history, a time when our nation, our churches, and American's of every stripe desperately need strong

---

[77] 1 Corinthians 1:26-31

Christian warriors to rush the battlefield. An Army of God fully outfitted with His courage cannot be defeated.

> Be strong and courageous, do not be afraid or tremble at them, for the LORD your God is the one who goes with you. He will not fail you or forsake you.[78]

> Wait for the LORD; Be strong and let your heart take courage; Yes, wait for the LORD.[79]

> Say to those with anxious heart, "Take courage, fear not. Behold, your God will come *with* vengeance; The recompense of God will come, But He will save you."[80]

> These things I have spoken to you, so that in Me you may have peace. In the world you have tribulation, but take courage; I have overcome the world."[81]

We are called to be warriors who live humble, dedicated, loyal, and righteous lives. Warriors train the next generation to live the same. Warriors demonstrate leadership and take authority over the enemy in Jesus name. Will you be numbered with the warriors?

---

[78] Deuteronomy 31:6
[79] Psalm 27:14
[80] Isaiah 35:4
[81] John 16:33

Final Thoughts

But I will raise up for Myself a faithful priest who will do according to what is in My heart and in My soul; and I will build him an enduring house, and he will walk before My anointed always. 1 Samuel 2:35

Of interest to many pastors, ministry leaders, and church support organizations is the rise in the number of people who consider themselves to be "nones" or "dones." The "nones" group is comprised of people who respond to questions related to religious affiliation with "none." The second group is comprised of people who are "done" with the Church as an institution. It is not my intention here to detail and discuss the myriad reasons for these responses. I mention them because I think they share a common root cause.

A large percentage of the nones have never darkened the door of a church. Their knowledge of Christianity is based solely on what they happen to observe on television or hear their friends and family discuss. The dones are on the other end of the spectrum. They for the most part have been raised in the Church and active in various roles while still professing faith in God even though they no longer attend any Church services. Many opt instead for home fellowships or other gatherings of believers in an informal setting.

What do these groups have in common? They both simply want a message that matters and neither group is hearing one from the Church writ large..

The nones among us are not necessarily anti-Christian. Indeed, spirituality is at an all-time high in America so there is a large percentage of seekers among the nones. Unfortunately the modern Church is more concerned with feeding God's people the latest self-help pop psychology wrapped in Christian garb than it is in teaching God's Word faithfully book by book and chapter by chapter in a systematic and comprehensive fashion. The competition is fierce in the self-help category with the likes of Oprah, Chopra, and Osteen carrying the day. No wonder nones aren't listening to the religious equivalent of this group of New Age icons.

The dones likewise long for a clear declaration of God's truth through a matter-of-fact exposition of the text. A large number of pastors have rejected a deep dive into the Scriptures and an equally challenging presentation of the biblical texts. Their weekly offering of the Word falls well short of being spiritual food and nourishment for God's people. God must be the focus of our exposition and Christ the answer to the issues we face. When the focus becomes people, their problems, and the steps they must take to regain their happy life, a concoction of spiritual poison has been brewed. Dispensed such a worldly elixir week after week will guarantee a Laodicean church.

King David declared in Psalm 19:7 that "the testimony of the LORD is sure, making wise the simple." This entire chapter is devoted to general (Psalm 19:1-6) and special (Psalm 19:7-13) revelation. The point in verse 8 is that God's Word is sure because it is trustworthy. It is trustworthy because it corresponds to reality. In other words, God's Word speaks with razor sharpness concerning our common human condition and provides the same clarity when it comes to the remedy He has provided for us.

Pastors, it is time to scale again the mountaintop of biblical exposition and declaration. God has called you to that task, He has supplied you with all you need to perform it, and the people He has entrusted to your care must have it. We are called to be theologians and shepherds not self-esteem masseuses or motivational coaches.

A major factor that keeps both the nones and dones disinterested in the church is the inability or outright refusal of God's shepherds to preach the Word of God without compromise. Unfortunately, this is nothing new and certainly not unexpected.

God states plainly through the prophet Amos for example that "days are coming… when I will send a famine on the land, not a famine for bread or a thirst for water, but rather for hearing the words of the LORD." (Amos 8:11)

Through the prophet Jeremiah God identified why this latter day famine would be so widespread: "Many shepherds have ruined My vineyard, They have trampled down My field; They have made My pleasant field a desolate wilderness" (Jeremiah 12:10)

> "Woe to the shepherds who are destroying and scattering the sheep of My pasture! Declares the LORD." Therefore thus says the LORD God of Israel concerning the shepherds who are tending My people: "You have scattered My flock and driven them away, and have not attended to them; behold, I am about to attend to you for the evil of your deeds," declares the LORD."[82]

> "My people have become lost sheep; Their shepherds have led them astray. They have made them turn aside *on* the mountains; they have gone along from mountain to hill and have forgotten their resting place."[83]

Through the prophet Ezekiel God spoke these words:

> "As I live," declares the Lord GOD, "surely because My flock has become a prey, My flock has even become food for all the beasts of the field for lack of a shepherd, and My shepherds did not search for My flock, but *rather* the shepherds fed themselves and did not feed My flock;"[84]

And then this:

> 'Thus says the Lord GOD, "Behold, I am against the shepherds, and I will demand My sheep from them and make them cease from feeding sheep. So the shepherds will not feed themselves anymore, but I will

[82] Jeremiah 23:1-2
[83] Jeremiah 50:6
[84] Ezekiel 34:8

deliver My flock from their mouth, so that they will not be food for them."[85]

I am willing to admit that some shepherds today simply do not know how to preach and to teach the Bible. Fifty plus years of inadequate and intentionally misguided seminary training has yielded a generation of shepherds ill-prepared to be the leaders of God's people that they must be.

However, there are a growing number of shepherds who simply choose not to teach God's Word. They have chosen to be CEO's instead of foot washers, public relations managers instead of holy writ counselors, and managers of staffs instead of friends to people in their fellowships.

To these God spoke as well: "Thus says the LORD, Stand by the ways and see and ask for the ancient paths, where the good way is, and walk in it; and you will find rest for your souls. But they said, 'We will not walk *in it*' and I set watchmen over you, *saying*, 'Listen to the sound of the trumpet!' But they said, 'We will not listen' (Jeremiah 6:16-17).

Friends, what all of these passages and many more speak of is the absolute necessity of God's shepherds knowing God's Word, being able to counsel using God's Word, and basing church life and practice on God's Word.

God has always set a clear path for His shepherds to lead His people upon. Today, many shepherds have chosen a path that appeals more to the flesh than to the spirit. When God's people are fed God's Word they will flourish. Perhaps the issue for modern day shepherds is a lack of faith and trust in the power of God's Word.

Don't mistake goat food for sheep food. Large crowds and large church campuses do not identify healthy ministries. Faithfulness to God and His revealed Word are the marks of a faithful shepherd and church. Now today more than ever, as the shepherd goes, so goes the sheep.

Pastor you must be a theologian because people are perishing without hearing the lifesaving message of salvation through faith in Christ while they are simultaneously entertained with stage props and warm-fuzzy motivational speeches about being better parents, spouses, students, or

---

[85] Ezekiel 34:10

employees. Moreover God has called and equipped you with His gifts to teach people His Word for the purpose of leading them to a deeper, richer, and more abundantly full relationship with Him. They will need this equipping when they face persecution for their faith.

Luke records for us these words of Jesus spoken to His disciples as He prepared them to go into all the land to preach, teach, and make disciples: "I will give you utterance and wisdom which none of your opponents will be able to resist or refute" (Luke 21:15). The context of this encouragement from our Lord was that faithfully preaching, teaching, and making disciples will result in persecution.

I am convinced that the reason so many pastors will not faithfully preach the Bible is because they have abandoned belief in its ability to save. Perhaps they have forgotten Paul's declaration that we are not to be ashamed of the Gospel of Jesus Christ because it is what God uses to bring people into His Kingdom. Paul calls the Gospel the power of God.

God has promised the power of the Holy Spirit to fuel the efforts of His work. It is the supreme privilege of the church to share God's amazing love and mercy to all who will believe on Jesus Christ. This simple message has become obscured today through a religious philosophy that suggests people must be made to feel welcome and comfortable in the church so that they will consider God's offer.

The critical problem with this approach is that it is not biblical. If the seeker sensitive era of church history has taught us anything it has taught us that it is bereft of the ability to make disciples of Jesus Christ. Bill Hybels, grandmaster of the seeker sensitive movement recently admitted this very thing and repented of the wasted years and effort that rendered little to no fruit.

Understanding this, what must be done to turn the tide? My personal view is that it is too late for the big "C" church as a whole. Many who hear this will disagree with this assessment. They hold out hope that we are not so late in God's timeline that things can't be turned around.

Nevertheless, we have arrived at the time of the remnant. We are past the tipping point. First, Pastor, be faithful where you are planted. Pour your best into the people God has entrusted to your care. Do not follow the way of those who advocate for a Wall Street approach to church growth. The entire church growth model is corrupt, worldly, and fleshly in that it is based on appealing to the felt needs of the lost. Trust Jesus to build His church as He desires it to be built. Jesus' keys to Kingdom success look nothing like what the church growth gurus are saying today.

Second, Pastors, trust God and His Word. Resist the temptation to twist the Bible into some kind of self-fulfillment manual. The Bible is God's message to His creation of His redemption, sanctification, and glorification of a people who trust in the finished work of Jesus Christ on Calvary's cross. Do not lose sight of the fact that the Gospel is the power of God to save.

Finally, Pastors - and this is equally applicable to every believer - focus your time and energy on making disciples. That is the last command of Jesus before He ascended to glory. Be a disciple who makes disciples for the glory of our King!

About the Author

Mike Spaulding was ordained to the ministry in 1998. Since then he has planted two Calvary Chapel churches - Calvary Christian Fellowship, St. Marys, Ohio, in 1998, and Calvary Chapel of Lima, Ohio, in 2005, where he currently serves as pastor.

Mike holds a B.A. in Organizational Management, a MTS in Theological Studies, and a Ph.D. in apologetics. He is the author of numerous articles including, "Leadership and Organizational Vision," "Servant Leadership," "The Ministry of Teaching," "A Brief Look At Romans 13," and "How and Why Should We Study the Bible." He is a contributing author to the soon to be released, *The Baker Dictionary of World Religions*, H. Wayne House, General Editor, and has just released his new book, *#MTPGA: 12 Things Christians Can Do Right Now*. Mike has written for several apologetics ministries including *Got Questions?* (www.gotquestions.org) and the *Christian Apologetics and Research Ministry* (www.carm.org) and maintains his own radio and podcast platforms – The Transforming Word (www.thetransformingword.com) Soaring Eagle Radio (www.soaringeagleradio.com) and his blog, Dr. Mike Spaulding (www.drmikespaulding.com)

His teaching ministry is featured on the radio program "The Transforming Word," heard on stations throughout the Midwest United States. He is the host of the radio and podcast show, Soaring Eagle Radio (www.soaringeagle.com), heard on Talk America Radio (www.talkamericaradio.us) , Global Star Radio Network (www.gsradio.net), Worldview Weekend Radio (www.worldvieweekend.com/radio) Prepper Broadcasting Network (www.prepperbroadcasting.com), The Fringe Radio Network (www.fringeradio.com), and WTTP FM (www.wttpfm.com) and available on all major subscription services including iTunes, Stitcher, TuneIn and On The Objective (www.ontheobjective.org).

Mike's professional memberships have included the Evangelical Philosophical Society, the International Society of Christian Apologetics, the Evangelical Theological Society, and the Evangelical Political Scholars Association. He serves on the board of directors of The Transforming Word Radio Ministries.

Mike has been married to his lovely wife Kathy for over 35 years and together they have four daughters and five grandchildren.

You may contact Mike via email – pastormike@cclohio.org or by writing him at the address below. You may follow him on Twitter - @ccpastormike or @soaringeaglerad

Dr. Mike Spaulding
Calvary Chapel of Lima
682 W. Grand Avenue
Lima, Ohio 45801

Bibliography

Boldea, Michael, Jr. *The Battle-Ready Believer.* Boldman Publishing, 2016.

Dalley, Stephanie. "Erra and Ishum IV," *Myths from Mesopotamia* (Oxford University Press, 1989.

Gurnall, William. *The Christian in Complete Armour.* The Banner of Truth Trust, 1989.

Hofner, Harry A. Jr., "Incest, Sodomy and Bestiaity in the Ancient Near East," in *Orient and Occident: Essays Presented to Cyrus H. Gordon on the Occasion of His Sixty-fifth Birthday,* ed. Harry A. Hoffner, Jr., Neukirchen Verlag, 1973.

Huxley, Aldoous. *Brave New World.* International Collectors Library, 1946.

Johnson, Ken. *Ancient Church Fathers: What the Disciples of the Apostles Taught* (Self Published, 2010.

Lindsell, Harold. *The Battle for the Bible.* Calvary Chapel Publishing, 2008.

Smith, Mark S., trans. *Ugaritic Narrative Poetry,* ed. Simon B. Parker. Society of Biblical Literature, 1997.

Tozer, A. W., and Ron Eggert. *Tozer on Christian Leadership: a 366-Day Devotional.* Christian Publications Inc., 2001.

Trewhella, Matthew. *The Doctrine of the Lesser Magistrates.* Createspace Independent Publishing Platform. 2013.